DENNIS MARUK

THE UNFORGETTABLE STORY
OF HOCKEY'S FORGOTTEN 60-GOAL MAN

Dennis Maruk *with* Ken Reid

Published by ECW Press
665 Gerrard Street East
Toronto, ON M4M 1Y2
416-694-3348 / info@ecwpress.com

Library and Archives Canada Cataloguing in Publication

Maruk, Dennis, 1955–, author
Dennis Maruk : the unforgettable story of hockey's forgotten 60-goal man / Dennis Maruk with Ken Reid; foreword by Marcel Dionne.

Issued in print and electronic formats.
ISBN 978-1-77041-331-3 (hardcover)
ISBN 978-1-77305-061-4 (PDF)
ISBN 978-1-77305-062-1 (EPUB)

1. Maruk, Dennis, 1955–. 2. Hockey players—Canada—Biography. I. Reid, Ken, 1974–, author II. Trottier, Bryan, writer of foreword III. Title.

GV848.5.M37A3 2017   796.962092   C2017-902403-5
C2017-902982-7

Editor for the press: Michael Holmes
Cover design: Michel Vrana
Cover images: courtesy Washington Capitals Photography
Interior images: from the author's personal collection, unless otherwise indicated.

The publication of *Dennis Maruk* has been generously supported by the Government of Canada through the Canada Book Fund. *Ce livre est financé en partie par le gouvernement du Canada.* We also acknowledge the contribution of the Government of Ontario through the Ontario Book Publishing Tax Credit and the Ontario Media Development Corporation.

Printed and bound in Canada
by: Friesens   5   4   3   2   1

I would like to dedicate this book to my three children, Jon, Sarah, and Jaylee. Their love and support has always helped me through my ups and downs.

All this would not have happened if I did not get the direction, dedication, and guidance from my parents, John and Anne. From the early years of my father making a rink in the backyard to my London Knights junior days when my mom and dad (parents of eight) drove back and forth, through sleet and snow, from Toronto to London for almost every game, my parents have always supported me. Mom, I miss you and you are always in my heart.

Contents . . .

Foreword by Marcel Dionne . . . VII

01 The Boat . . . 1
02 The White/Black/Grey Elephant in the Room . . . 4
03 Hating Hockey . . . 8
04 Reality Bites . . . 13
05 London Calling . . . 17
06 This Is Easy . . . 21
07 Where's Maruk? . . . 24
08 Learn to Be a Prick . . . 26
09 A Whole Lotta Boom Boom . . . 30
10 This Is the NHL? . . . 35
11 No, This Is the NHL? . . . 41
12 Veteran Advice . . . 45
13 You Still Owe Me! . . . 47
14 Hello, Cleveland . . . 51
15 Hot News . . . 54
16 Liquid Lunch and a Hockey Game . . . 58
17 Nobody Dreams of the Barons . . . 62
18 Minnesota or Bust — I'll Take Bust . . . 67
19 Hello, Goodbye . . . 70
20 Capital City . . . 74
21 Mr. International . . . 78
22 A New Dad . . . 86
23 Guitar Town . . . 90
24 Chasing 50 . . . 93
25 The Same Old Situation . . . 96
26 Finding My Groove . . . 99
27 Mr. President . . . 103
28 Shivers . . . 107
29 The Road to 60 . . . 110

30 60 ... 113

31 Go Ovie ... 117

32 Maruk and Oates ... 121

33 Save the Caps ... 125

34 The Left Side ... 129

35 The Caps Are Hot ... 133

36 The Christians and the Lions ... 136

37 A Very Short Debut ... 139

38 Back to Minny ... 143

39 Survival of the Prickiest ... 146

40 A Five-Year Loan ... 150

41 Cowbell ... 153

42 A Glimmer of the Past ... 155

43 Lessons from a Coach and a Baby Girl ... 159

44 Ouch ... 166

45 I'm Done ... 170

46 Now What? ... 175

47 The Art of Scoring ... 178

48 One Door Opens, Another Closes ... 184

49 The WPHL ... 186

50 The Comeback ... 189

51 The Boat, Part II ... 192

52 So Long, Louisiana ... 195

53 Rocky Mountain High ... 197

54 Broken ... 200

55 Driving to Death ... 203

56 Home ... 209

57 Mom ... 215

58 Thank You ... 220

59 What Does 60 Mean? ... 225

60 Now ... 228

Acknowledgements ... 237

FOREWORD

by Marcel Dionne

I first heard about a player named Dennis Maruk when I was in the NHL and he was racking up the points in junior with the London Knights. He ended up with 145 points in his final year of junior, two more than my single junior season-high — something he would remind me about when he eventually made it to the NHL.

Dennis was a lot like me. We weren't the biggest players in the league, but he was a very competitive guy. We didn't play for very good teams either. It's not that our teams had bad players, we just weren't on good teams. When he came up as a rookie with the Seals, all I would see was a pretty quiet guy who was scoring goals behind that Fu Machu. But when I got the chance to play with Dennis at the World Championships, I saw a different side of him. And it's that side of Dennis that helped him to have an impressively long career, playing in the NHL for 14 seasons, in almost 900 regular-season games.

They used to call Dennis "Pee Wee." Well, that word doesn't exist in my life. A lot of hockey teams will visit my diner in Niagara Falls. I always meet the teams when they come in, and the first thing I always ask is, "Who is the smallest player here?" All the kids will point to the guy right away. Little guys are very well liked — they have energy; they have something special. I will ask the kid his name and I'll tell him that there is no such thing as being small. That is something that Dennis and I proved throughout our NHL careers. We played in a high flying and tough era, and even though we weren't the biggest guys on the ice, it didn't matter.

In the winter of 2017, I was named to the NHL's 100 Greatest Players of All Time. I was chatting with Eric Lindros and Chris Pronger when the Top 100 were revealed. I said, "Boy, I would have loved to have played against you guys."

And Chris Pronger, who was really quick with his response, said, "You would have gone right through our legs, eh."

And I said, "You're exactly right."

Here's the thing: I will walk in to a room with Eric Lindros, who is 6-foot-5 and 245 pounds. I'm 5-foot-7 and a half. I'm a little heavier now than in my playing days, but let's say I'm 185, 190 pounds. People look at me beside Eric in amazement. I'll say this: Eric is a German shepherd; he's big and he's strong. But Dennis and I are pit bulls. Well, guess what? The German shepherd might bite you once, but then he'll quit. The pit bull, however, won't quit. Dennis Maruk was a pit bull who scored 60 goals in an NHL season. It's time you heard his story.

1 THE BOAT

I peered out the window. My eyes searched for any sign of the sky, but there was nothing. The only thing I could see was wave after wave crashing into the thin pane of glass that separated me from an impromptu swim. And I wanted absolutely no part of that.

"Dennis, take over the boat," the captain said. The captain was older and smaller than me. A nice man and a veteran sailor who had spent 30 years on the sea, he was skinny and missing a few teeth. He clearly looked the part.

Take over the boat? What in the hell was this guy talking about? We were in the middle of the Gulf of Mexico, surrounded by massive oil tankers, and, trust me, this was not the night to be out for a pleasure cruise.

"I've gotta get some sleep," the captain said.

The boat was a 160-foot-long supply ship. The mission: deliver supplies to tankers throughout the Gulf of Mexico. However, my mission on this night was a bit different: survive. There were two deck hands and two captains on board. One crew was asleep, and my captain and I were at the helm. For some strange reason, the captain thought it was the perfect time to throw me, a greenhorn, to the wolves . . . or was it the fishes? "I'm tired. I'm going to lie down. You run the ship." Those were the captain's orders.

I guess I didn't have much of a choice. Before he climbed into his bunk, the captain gave me one final tap on the shoulder. I looked up from the computer-controlled monitors and into the captain's eyes, ready for my one and only lesson before I took control of the ship.

"There's one thing you gotta look out for on the radar," he bellowed. "THE BIG WHITE BARS. Those are the rigs, the big oil containers, and the boats. Wake me up when you see one of those."

He told me not to worry, everything was on radar. Well, he said, almost everything — there might be the odd ship that hadn't been registered. Gee, that's comforting — just the odd ship that I can't see as wave after wave crashes into us in the dead of the night. I can handle that — on my third day on the job. (Yes, I'm being sarcastic.)

With that, the captain was off to bed. Waves were crashing around me, the boat was tumbling from one side to the other, and I was the only guy awake on the ship. For the first few minutes behind the helm, my heart was pounding. I wanted to quit. I couldn't do this. But quitting was not an option.

I looked over at the captain, who was nodding off. I asked, "How long are you going to sleep?" I figured he'd say a couple of minutes. Instead, he just looked over at me and said, "A couple of hours."

And just like that, I was a boat captain on the high seas, navigating through the night — and through life.

Just a few years earlier, sailing the high seas was not part of my future plans. After all, I was dining with the president of the United States, on my way to becoming just the seventh man in NHL history to score 60 goals in a season. But life had delivered its fair share of surprises, and there would be many more to come.

My name is Dennis Maruk, and this is my story.

2 THE WHITE/BLACK/ GREY ELEPHANT IN THE ROOM

"Dennis had one of the best Fu Manchus in the league. Today, he sometimes still tries to grow it, except it's grey. He led the '70s look in the league. It would have been noticed more, but he was in Washington."

— Wendel Clark, Leafs legend

Before we go any further, let's address one thing right off the bat — my moustache. These days, when I show up at a charity hockey game or at any other function where I'm part of the festivities, the first question I usually get once I enter the room is, "Hey, Maruk! Where's the moustache?"

Based on that question, I'm sure you can conclude that the "Moustache" is not around anymore. But I wore it for my entire playing career. When I scored 60 goals, it was there. When I met the president, it was there. When I showed up in Oakland, it was there. And on all my hockey cards, it's there. You didn't see the

Capitals on *Hockey Night in Canada* very often back in the day, but if you opened a pack of O-Pee-Chee hockey cards in 1982, you knew the Caps had a guy with a wicked handlebar. Well, that was me. So let's get to the bottom of how I became known as the man with the Fu Manchu.

When I was 14 years old, I got my first summer job. I didn't work at a burger joint, or pump gas, or help out at a farm like a lot of hockey players did. I bought liquor. Yep. My first summer job as a kid in Toronto was going on liquor runs for other kids. How did I get the gig? The answer is simple. Not only was I blessed with an ability to play the game of hockey, but I was also blessed with the ability to grow a beard at a very young age. They are two unique talents, one perhaps just a bit more profitable than the other.

This is how the Fu came about. One summer day, I was watching a baseball game on television. Into my sights came a pitcher named Al Hrabosky. He was a hard-throwing lefty known as "the Mad Hungarian." Not only did he have a unique handle, but he had a unique handlebar as well. This dude sported the thickest moustache I had ever seen. He was going nuts on the mound. He was a mad man and I remember thinking to myself, *Oh shit, I gotta grow the Fu Manchu.* So I did, and I kept it throughout my entire hockey career.

The Fu made me look a little meaner than I was, maybe a little tougher than I was, and definitely a lot older than I was. It made me look old enough that I could go for liquor runs when I was barely into my teens. I would walk in with dirty jeans and a dirty T-shirt. I'd look like I had just come off a work site and was getting a few for my buddies. I'd walk in with work boots on and a hat and the 'stache. Now, you may think a guy who looked like this would go for a case of Molson Stock Ale or Old Vienna. Not me. I'd reach for the nearest bottle of lemon gin. That's what my friends and I used to drink.

Of course, if I was risking life and limb by going to the nearest liquor store for the boys, I'd make money off the deal. I'd take their order, make the purchase, and my friends would tip me out. It was a sweet gig.

And here's the thing. I never got asked for ID. That Fu Manchu served me well. It made me look meaner on the ice and it got me an all-access card into any adult-beverage store. I think the first time I ever got asked for ID was just a couple of years ago. It was at a pub in Ottawa during the All-Star Game. They checked everybody going in. I was thinking, *You've got to be kidding me.* But I didn't have the Fu Manchu at the time. I told you it makes me look older.

I shaved the thing off a few years ago; it just didn't feel right anymore. Back in the day, though, it was my trademark. I think it still is. "Hey, there's Maruk, the 60-goal guy . . . you know, the guy with the Fu Manchu!"

Right before my first team picture with the California Golden Seals, the boys made me shave the Fu into a little Hitler moustache. It was my initiation, and it looked horrible. It took about a week, but it grew back. Not everything sprang back to life, though. The boys didn't just stop at the 'stache, they also shaved my eyebrows off, which were never able to make the comeback that my moustache did. I used to have real thick eyebrows. Not anymore. Now they look terrible.

I wanted that Fu Manchu on the ice. The boys may have

thought shaving most of it off was funny, but my Fu helped me find my identity in the game. I was small. And like I said, it made me look just a little tougher. As a player, if you think something helps you, then it helps you. I have Al Hrabosky to thank for making me feel bigger.

I was mean on the ice. I was never a happy camper out there — I had a great time but I was stubborn. And if I had two goals, I wanted a third one, and I would do whatever it took to get number three. Sure, the Fu was a point of style, but it was much more than that. It was part of what made me believe I could go into a corner against a guy who had eight inches and 45 pounds on me and come out with the puck.

I gave up on the Fu for a while in Cleveland and went with a big thick beard, but it just didn't work. My teammates all kind of looked at me, wondering where the Fu went. "That's you," they said. "Bring back the Fu. Keep it, keep it."

I'd like to think that Lanny McDonald and I rocked the best moustaches in hockey history. And since I'd like to use this book not only to share my story but also to educate, here's my quick four-step guide on how to grow a Fu that will make you a much better player both on and off the ice.

1. Grow a beard.
2. Shave beard into a goatee.
3. Shave the middle of the goatee under the bottom lip.
4. Keep the 'stache a good inch and a half wide on each side.

Voila! Enjoy your Fu Manchu.

3 HATING HOCKEY

"In our neighbourhood, the next-door neighbour had three boys and there were a couple of kids down the street, so we were constantly on the road playing ball hockey. Dennis commentated as we played — everybody was a different NHL player."

— Ken Maruk, Dennis's little brother

You know all those hockey stories out there about a young boy lacing up his first pair of skates, taking his first strides on a beautiful frozen pond with snowflakes falling from the sky on a beautiful winter's day? You do? Good.

Now get rid of that image because that sure as hell wasn't me.

I grew up in Rexdale, a nice little neighbourhood in Toronto's west end. I had seven brothers and sisters. The chain went like this, from youngest to oldest, Donna, Karen, Peter, me, Barry, Linda, Kenny, and Lori. Being good Canadian kids, of course we played hockey. These days, you see parents getting their kids out

The Maruk kids with Mom and Dad. That's me on the far right.

on the ice as soon as they can walk. Maybe a lot of them hope they are looking at a future NHLer. I didn't hit the ice until I was six years old, and I absolutely hated it. If you had told me that I would play hockey for a living, my six-year-old self would have had no part in it — the tears on my face would have shown you that.

My dad, John, made a little ice rink in our backyard. Wanting to be like my older brother and sisters, I decided that I needed skates to take part in Maruk family activities. I took to our little backyard oasis for all of 10 seconds. Too cold and unbalanced, I cried, "I'm not doing this," and I didn't for the next two years. While all the other kids in my family and neighbourhood were out skating and playing hockey, I was more than happy to leave life on the ice to them.

For me, hockey was best played on the road, not on ice. Ball hockey was the number one wintertime activity in Rexdale, and I loved it. It was all hands — and no skates. There were no pucks, only tennis balls. What could be better? Our street wasn't all that busy in the winter, so we had a perfect place to play. Once in a while a car would come by, and being good Canadian kids, we'd halt the game to let them through. Then it was game on again. That was hockey for me; I forgot all about the ice.

When I was eight years old, my buddy Kevin Blackey, who lived two doors down, wanted to see how I would fare with a puck. I scored a lot of goals on the road with a tennis ball. But Kevin, our resident goalie, wanted to see if I could shoot a puck. He took his spot in the crease, and I took my spot a good 20 feet in front of him and lined up a few pucks. I let the first one rip. It breezed by Kevin and into the net. The same for shot number two. Shot three found the net as well. Kevin was impressed. So was I. I was getting more confident by the second. I ripped into another puck — it accelerated toward the net. And it was rising, headed right for Kevin. He was about to stop me for the first time. But he didn't want to. The puck hit him right in the family jewels — and his jewels were not protected that day. He was down, wailing. I thought he was going to be sick. I was in shock. I had no idea what I had done until he screamed, "I didn't have my jock on." I simply stated, "Oh shit."

My first-ever house-league team. I'm in the front row just to the right of our goalie.

His parents quickly arrived on the scene and took the young goaltender right to the hospital. A few hours later, I went over to his place to see him. He said he was going to be a little bruised and sore for the next couple of days. Then he added, "You shoot the puck really well." It was time for me to move from the road to the ice.

My transition to the ice was easy. In my first year of organized hockey, I led our league in scoring. The next year, I joined a rep team and never looked back. My game just took off — during all my minor-hockey years, I was near or at the top of my team and league in scoring. I never really gave it much thought. I just loved playing the game, and I loved to score goals — maybe a little too much. If a goalie made a save or I didn't score, I would slam my stick against the boards. I had a hell of a temper and I got benched a bunch of times.

As I got older, the goals kept coming, and my temper cooled — at least a little bit. By the time I was 14, I was playing Junior B and dreaming of playing for the Toronto Maple Leafs. My life was going according to plan — until, that is, it came off the rails in the summer of '72.

4 REALITY BITES

"He was traded to the Knights and he was only 16 years old. He just said, 'Sis, the Marlies traded me to London. I can't go. This is home.' I told him it was the opportunity of a lifetime, 'You'll never get this opportunity again.'"

— Karen Courville, Dennis's sister

No one really wants to get traded. Okay, sure, if you make a request to be moved, that's another story, but an out-of-the-blue see-you-later is never the sort of thing that makes your day. Most hockey players learn of the no holds barred cut-throat business of a hockey trade once they become pros. I was first introduced to this side of the game in the summer of 1972.

I was 16 years old. In my eight games with the Ontario Hockey Association's Toronto Marlies the previous spring, I put up two goals and one assist for three points. Small numbers, but they were just a start. After all, I was a kid and the future looked bright. And my future, I thought, was in Marlies blue and white. I was wrong.

The Metro Junior B All Stars. Mike Palmateer is front row left. The other goalie is Gary Carr, who was eventually drafted by the Bruins. My future NHL teammate Rick Hampton is the first player on the left in the second row. I'm second from the left in the back row. Just left of me is Bruce Boudreau.

One of my teammates on the Marlies was Marty Howe. Well, great hockey powers wanted Marty's brother Mark on the Marlies as well, and those hockey powers were Mr. and Mrs. Hockey. Gordie and Colleen Howe wanted their boys to play junior together. Lucky me — I was the guy who made it possible. Actually, there were three of us. Steve Langdon and Larry Goodenough were also involved in the trade that brought Mark from the London Knights to the Toronto Marlies.

The Marlies originally offered Bruce Boudreau in the deal, but the Knights said no. They wanted me. I'll never forget hearing the news. I was at a corner gas station on my way to play in a lacrosse game. Devastated isn't a strong enough word. I got back in the car and cried. In fact, I wept all the way to the lacrosse game. I dreamed of having a junior career with the Marlies and it was over after eight games. I played lacrosse that day, but I couldn't tell you who won or who lost. My mind was elsewhere and my heart was crushed. After the game, I went home and talked to my parents about the deal. I could reach only one conclusion: I was going to quit. I said, "I'm staying in Toronto. I'm not going to London." I remember telling my parents that if Bill Long, the head coach of the Knights, called, they should tell him to make another trade. "I'm not going. Tell him I'm staying in Toronto." I was finished with hockey.

I was 16 years old, basically a kid, but I was at a crossroads. The trade created a *What do I want to do with my life?* internal dialogue. I loved hockey, but I didn't love the situation I found myself in. Sure, I wanted to play, but I didn't want to pack up my bags and leave my friends at such a young age. I had just come out of Junior B, I was the leading scorer, and we had won the championship. We won everything. And now it was Marlies time. That was always the plan for me, and I just couldn't wrap my mind around the trade. Why would they trade me? Why didn't the Marlies want me? The summer of 1972 was a very emotional time for me and my entire family.

That summer, Bill Long did everything he could to try to convince me to report to London. He had made about three or four trips into town to visit my family. He could tell I was disappointed and angry. As soon as he'd come over, I'd just leave the house. Bill would talk to my parents, he'd tell them that the Knights would take care of me, but he never said a word to me.

How could he? As soon as I saw him I would bolt. I spent my summer playing baseball and lacrosse. I decided that I didn't really want to play hockey.

I stuck to my guns for the entire summer. I was not going. About two weeks before training camp, I was talking with my older sister Karen. She said, "Go. If you like it, stay; and if not, quit and come back home. Your call." Damn, I did love the game, and I was miserable thinking about a year without hockey.

After much thought and with my sister's wise words playing in my head, I decided I'd give it a try. But I had a few stipulations for Bill Long before I headed west on the 401. First and foremost: no one touches my hair! I had pretty long hair at the time; I used to even wear it in a ponytail on some days. If I was going to London, my hair was going with me and it was staying. I was going to be a first-year player on the team, but my hair would not be sacrificed as part of my initiation onto the Knights. Long spread the word: "Don't touch Maruk's hair." No one did.

Stipulation number two: no one touches my moustache. Again, Long spread the word: "Don't touch the moustache." No one did.

And just like that, I was a London Knight. What a negotiator.

5 LONDON CALLING

"The couple was very nice, but it was just them. Dennis used to tell me that they used to sit and watch him eat. My folks took him in and I think it was a little bit more like his house, kind of crazy, and we had fun. I think it felt more like home to him."

— Joni Butzow, Dennis's first wife

I was a Knight, but there was no love at first sight with London. I missed home, a lot.

I missed my friends and, of course, I missed my mom and dad. I must say, my mother and father were absolutely tremendous during my first season and for my entire junior career with the Knights. If they could make it to a game, they would be there. Mom and Dad would get into their car and make the drive from the west end of Toronto to most, if not all, of my home games. When the game was over, they'd hop back in the car and make the two-hour drive back to Toronto. If we were on the road in Kitchener, my parents were there. If we were on the road in Oshawa, they would be there. The only games Mom and Dad didn't make it to were the ones way up north in either Sudbury or Sault Ste. Marie. They drove through everything: wind, sleet, snow. I can't thank my parents enough for what they did.

It meant everything to me to see them at my games, in part because I was away from home and in part because I had no one to speak to at my billet's house in London. And I mean no one. Well, I could speak, but no one could understand me. The Knights had me living with a German family. They spoke very little English. One thing that was not lost in translation, however, was the fact that I needed to gain weight.

When I joined the Knights, I weighed 150 pounds. That's not ideal when you're going into the corners against OHA defencemen like, oh, let's say, Denis Potvin. The Knights wanted a much bigger version of me, and they must have given the orders to my billet family.

Upon moving in, I was immediately introduced to the largest meals my eyes had ever seen. These things were huge. Three huge pork chops or steaks would be thrown in front of me. I would eat it all, or at least try to; if I didn't down what was in front of me, my billet family would call Bill Long and tell them that I had not consumed all of their delicious offerings. Welcome to off-ice nutrition circa 1972. The team was giving the Germans money to feed me, and they wanted to get their money's worth. I don't think it worked.

They not only constantly called the coach about my eating habits, but they also called the coach about my social life as well. If I was out with the boys for even a second after curfew, they would be on the phone with the coach. The same thing happened when I was out on a date. One second after curfew and the coach's phone would be ringing off the hook.

A part of me thinks I was breaking curfew and partying as an act of rebellion against my situation. I was with a family I hardly knew, who was ordering me to down massive amounts of food, and, let's face it, a big part of me still wanted to be back in Toronto.

I mostly hung out with the older guys on the team. I was the rookie, but I was always hanging out with Larry Goodenough, Reg Thomas, Andy Spruce, and John Held. Those guys were old enough to get into the bars, and I *looked* old enough. We hung out at a bar called Hooks, not all that far from the rink.

Of course, if we were there in the afternoon, I would have to head back to my billet's for dinner and eat my three pork chops and four chicken legs. I spent as little time as possible at that house. That's why I would get into trouble. The coach would call to see if I was in for curfew, but I'd be out with Larry and the boys.

And I'd get in trouble at school as well. The principal would call the coach asking where I was. I'd go to school maybe two or three days a week. The Knights made me meet with the principal to discuss my truancy. He suggested I attend three or four classes. He told me I would meet people and make friends, but I didn't; I might have made one friend at school during my years in London. My teammates were my friends; they were my go-to people.

Eventually, I decided enough was enough. I stayed with the Germans for one year and then I moved out. No more pork chops for me.

Luckily, there were a couple of things in London that kept me sane. Things started to work out on the ice, and, perhaps just as important, things started to work out off the ice. For a teenage boy, I'm sure you know what that means: I met a girl. Her name was Joni and she was Ms. London Knight.

During my second year with the Knights, I moved in with Joni and her family. The coach was on the hunt for a new billet family for me and suggested I go live with my girlfriend's family until they found me a suitable replacement for the Germans. I ended up staying in a bedroom in Joni's family's basement. I stayed there for about a year and a half. Joni and I were eventually engaged and then married.

6 THIS IS EASY

"Dennis was a determined little bastard. He wanted to score. And any guy who wants to score is going to be successful. And I think being traded from the Marlies drove Dennis to want to be the player that he was and show them they screwed up."

— Terry Martin, London Knights linemate

If German pork chops and Ms. London Knight were all new to me, one thing that was familiar in London was the game itself. The turmoil I faced off the ice didn't seem to affect my on-ice performance. The Knights wanted a beefier version of me, but what they got was the same old skinny kid who could put the puck in the net.

The Knights put Terry Martin on my left wing. Terry went on to play 479 games in the NHL with Buffalo, Toronto, Minnesota, Quebec, and Edmonton. Terry and I were just a couple 16-year-olds, but we clicked. Bill Long kept us as a duo and would mix in a different right-winger on our line.

Terry and I basically stayed together for my entire three years in London. We gelled. If I scored, he set me up. If he scored, I set him up.

In my rookie year, I finished third on the Knights and ninth in league scoring with 113 points in 59 games. I was named the OHA's Rookie of the Year. The good times continued during my second season with the Knights. I led the Knights with 112 points in 69 games. Those numbers were good enough for eighth in the league scoring-race. At around this time, the possibility of a pro career was very much on my mind. There was just one problem: my size. But there wasn't a thing I could do about it. It didn't seem to matter what I did on the ice, I was always defined by my size. Even if I scored against an NHL team, the reaction seemed to be, "Who's the little guy?"

The Washington Capitals held their training camp in London one year. We played them in an exhibition game. I think we lost 8–5. I'd scored three or four goals against the Caps, and I'm sure they were looking at me and thinking, *This little guy is scoring goals on us.* That was before my second year in junior. When I went out and had another 100-plus-point season, I thought I was going to be drafted. But I wasn't. I was passed over at 18 because I was deemed too small for the NHL.

Bummer.

It wasn't as if the Knights weren't trying to make me look bigger. In the team program, I was listed at 5-foot-10 or 5-foot-11. Considering I'm 5-foot-8, that's pretty funny. Outside of the dressing room, one of the scouts had marked off five feet to six feet on a wall. I came out and just kind of laughed. To make matters worse, I slouched as I skated, so I looked even smaller.

I dealt with it by playing the best hockey I possibly could. My third year with the Knights was the most productive of my OHA career. In 65 games, I had 66 goals and I added 79 assists for 145 points. I was honoured to win the Red Tilson Award as the Most Valuable Player in the OHA.

I truly loved my time in London. I went there reluctantly, and I left a happy young man. In 2014, the *London Free Press* named their top 50 Knights of all time. I finished fifth on the list behind Corey Perry, Dino Ciccarelli, Darryl Sittler, and Brendan Shanahan. That's pretty good company. They are all NHL Hall of Famers. I'm followed on the list by Rick Nash, Rob Ramage, and Patrick Kane.

7 WHERE'S MARUK?

"It's a shame Dennis's jersey is not up in the rafters. No disrespect to some of those players who are up there, but Dennis was one of the all-time great London Knights."

— Terry Martin

These days, the only place you'll find my name in London is in the history books. I left the Knights as the team's all-time leading scorer with 370 points in 191 games. Corey Perry is now number one with 380 points. I'll be honest, though, I wouldn't mind if I was easier to find in London's arena.

When you head to a Knights game and look up at the ceiling, you will see several retired numbers hanging from the rafters. Dino is up there and so is Shanny, Rob Ramage, and Rick Nash. Perry, Sittler, and David Bolland are honoured, too. But my name is not up there and I'm not sure why.

Did I do something wrong during my time with the Knights? I don't think I said anything to offend a reporter or anything like that . . . I don't know, maybe it's because I didn't want to go to

London at first. But I had a great time there, and I still visit. A couple of years ago there was some talk that maybe a banner would go up . . . but nothing has happened yet.

I still look at some of my old Knights photos and smile — me with the long hair. And there's one of me with my teeth knocked out, and my face is so swollen that I had to wear a football mask. I had heard that a few folks in London presented a letter to team GM Basil McRae and owner Dale Hunter about my number being honoured, but I never heard anything more. When all the rumours about my banner going up were making the rounds, I even called the team. I wanted to make arrangements to get my family and friends there. "I hear my banner is going up. Is that true?" I said. They told me they had been talking about it, but nothing had been finalized and they'd call me. Like I said, I haven't heard from them.

Now, why do I care about a banner being raised to the roof in London? There are a number of factors, but first and foremost is my dad. He's over 90 years old now and still as fit as a fiddle. He's a quiet guy who doesn't say much, but I sure would like to take him to a ceremony like that just to say thank you for all he did for me during my hockey career. I would really be honoured. When I told my dad a few years ago that my banner might go up, he was really excited. He still asks me about London and about the banner, but I just tell him, "Sorry, Dad, I haven't heard anything from them yet." And he just tells me, "Dennis, that would be really special."

Do I lose sleep over the fact that I don't have a banner in London? No. Would I love to have one? Yes. I'm pretty sure it will happen. I just hope it's sooner rather than later.

8 LEARN TO BE A PRICK

"I do remember that conversation; it was at the London Gardens. It was a tough league back then. That was when they condoned fighting — they don't do that anymore. But that's the way you had to play back then — nasty — and Dennis did and he had a great career. For a little guy to score goals like that, it was amazing."

— Dave Hutchison, 1,550 PIM in 584 NHL games

With three OHA seasons under my belt and armed with the 1974–75 Red Tilson Award, I was pretty sure that it was my time. Despite my size, I was confident I would be drafted to the NHL.

The hype machine back then was minimal at best. In 1975, NHL prospects weren't hounded by the media all year long; I didn't appear on any "Prospect Watch" lists, and I didn't have my very own pre- pre-pre-rookie card. I was just a teenage kid hoping to get a phone call welcoming me to the NHL.

The 1975 NHL Entry Draft was held at the NHL offices in Montreal. It was not televised, and I was not there. I was at home waiting for the phone to ring. Despite the numbers I put up in the OHA, I was not the most confident kid when the draft rolled around. All the big-time prospects had the number one agent in the game, Alan Eagleson. I was not one of Eagleson's clients. He never asked me to come to his camp, so I didn't think I was worthy of such a big-time agent. Instead, I was with a group of lawyers out of Montreal and they assigned me an agent. My agent was one of the best hockey players of all time: Bernie "Boom Boom" Geoffrion. I knew Boom Boom could cut it on the ice, but my question was: could he cut it in the boardroom?

On draft day, I waited and waited for my name to be called. And I kept waiting. I remember looking at my watch and thinking the first round had to be in the books, and I was still waiting. I was not a first-rounder. Soon enough, though, the phone rang and I got the news. I was told I was drafted in the second round, 21st overall, by the California Golden Seals. "Great. Super. Looking forward to it."

The first thing I did was try to figure out where in the hell Oakland was, and then I tried to learn a little bit about the California Golden Seals. If you know anything at all about the Golden Seals, it is likely this: they wore white skates and they were not very good. I missed the white skates era, but I would get to experience the "not very good" thing.

After I had comfortably learned the basic history of my new team, the next step was getting a contract. That was not going to be easy. Boom Boom told me I was invited to camp but that I would not be going there with a contract. The Seals held their training camp in Portland, Oregon.

I had a couple of months to get ready; I was determined to make the Seals and start my pro career. I hit the ice whenever and wherever I could. It was during that summer that I learned the most valuable lesson about surviving in the pro game. It came directly from a pro, and it is not something I suggest you employ in your weekly beer-league game. Still, it was something I needed to master to survive as an undersized player in the extremely rough and unpredictable world of the mid-1970s NHL. The message: *learn to be a prick.*

One day, I bumped into Dave Hutchison. He was a 23-year-old former London Knight from Dorchester, Ontario. Dave had started his career in the Eastern League, climbed up to the WHA, and played in 68 games with the L.A. Kings during the 1974–75 season. Dave knew me and he knew I could score goals, but there was much more to the pro game. I asked him, "How do you make it in the NHL?"

He looked at me and said, "You can score goals, you can make plays, but you gotta be a prick."

I looked at him, stunned. "What do you mean?"

"You gotta run guys. You gotta hit guys," Dave said. "Because you're going to get hit. And you still gotta do your job. When you do that, you'll make more room for yourself. You're gonna have to fight. You're going to have to spear. You're going to have to slash. You're going to have to do all that stuff. I'm sure it's something you're probably not used to because you didn't have to do that in junior. But in pro, you're going to have to do it."

I had just been given a verbal NHL survival guide from a guy who was already in the Show. I was not going to question Dave

Hutchison. He had been there and knew how to survive. I was going to take his word as gospel.

Dave told me that when you go to camp, you have to hit everyone. It doesn't matter if they are the best players on your team — hit them. He told me I had to be aggressive. I had to be a shit disturber.

I didn't take any crap in junior. I'd hit back, but I was more focused on scoring goals than being a little prick out on the ice. If I was going to follow through on what Dave had said, I was going to have to take my aggressiveness to a whole new level. I decided to keep on scoring and dial up my prick meter a notch — maybe several notches.

9 A WHOLE LOTTA BOOM BOOM

"I had played against Dennis in junior, so I knew who he was coming in. I knew he was a little guy, but he was a tough little guy. He didn't get pushed around, and in front of the net he was deadly."

— Rick Hampton, California and Cleveland teammate

The first thing I did when I hit the ice at Seals camp was hit everything in sight. I didn't care who you were. Like Dave Hutchison had said, "You gotta hit everybody." I was letting the veteran guys like Dave Gardner, Larry Patey, and Bob Stewart know that I wanted a spot on the team. Remember, I didn't have a contract, so I was going all out. I'd hit anybody who was on the ice; I didn't care who they were. And if someone slashed me, I'd just slash them right back. That's the way it was. The guy I was feeding the wood to might be my teammate in a couple of weeks, but he wasn't yet. I wanted to be on that team, and if I had to master the art of being a prick to get on the roster, so be it.

One thing I learned very early in my first training camp with the California Golden Seals was that this was one relaxed, and I mean very relaxed, group. Training camps were nothing more than a luxury or hassle for the vets — depending on how you look at it — and it's possible my intensity was ticking off a few of them. For the vets, training camp was a time to get back in shape and, perhaps equally as important, a time to get reacquainted with the boys after a long summer off. California Golden Seals training camp in 1975 was one big party where the beer flowed freely. I remember thinking, *This is the NHL?*

First off, most of the guys came to camp overweight, some as much as 30 pounds. I was out there weighing 158 pounds and buzzing around like a madman while everyone else was just going for a leisure skate. Some guys at well above their playing weight could barely skate at all.

After practice on day two, everyone hit the bar. *Seriously?* But hey, what was I going to do? I was a rookie — I went out with the boys. Guys couldn't get to the bar fast enough after the skate. It was absolutely crazy. I thought, *There's no way every team in the league is like this.* Montreal had to be different, right? Toronto? But I heard all kinds of crazy stories about all of the teams back then. This was the mid-'70s NHL, and I was gunning to be a part of it. The daily schedule went like this: skate-party-rinse-wash-repeat. To be honest, things pretty much stayed that way until conditioning became a serious part of the game following the 1980 Miracle on Ice.

Camp eventually shifted down to Salt Lake City, and it was the same format. Hit the ice and then the bar. A lot of the guys on the Seals had spent time in the minors in Salt Lake City, so they knew where the blonde Mormon girls hung out. Camp was costing me money, too. One night, Ralph Klassen, who was another rookie on the team, and I got stuck with the bill. And let me tell you, the Seals weren't hanging out at joints with cheap booze and food. Ralph and I had to cough up around four grand.

Between all the skating and "team bonding," we did manage to sneak in some exhibition games. It was my chance to show the management that they made an excellent choice with the 21st overall pick in the 1975 NHL Draft. It was my chance to show the California Golden Seals that I belonged in the best hockey league in the world.

Our first exhibition game in the fall of 1975 was against our in-state rivals, the Los Angeles Kings. I was going to be lining up against a skilled guy who was on the smaller side, kind of like me. His name was Marcel Dionne. I really admired the way he played, and he pushed me to be better. I grew up worshipping Bobby Hull as a kid, then Marcel came around in the early '70s. He inspired me. *If he can do it, I can do it,* I thought.

I had a great game and scored a couple of goals. I think I may have even been first star, but I'm a little foggy about that. But I do know this: Right after the game, Bill McCreary, the Seals GM, and Munson Campbell, the team president, gave me a tap on the shoulder. That night's performance against the Kings was enough to show the Seals that I was big-league material. They told me to pack up my stuff and get back to Oakland to sign a contract. Now it was time for some shrewd Boom Boom negotiating. Boom Boom had already been going at the duo since the start of training camp.

Before camp started, Boom Boom and I had met with the

Seals upper brass and talked a little turkey. "Well, my Dennis," Boom Boom had told McCreary and company in his French accent, "he score you a lot of goals. So we sign contract right now." When I heard Boom Boom make his demand, I burst out laughing. I wasn't much of a negotiator but I wasn't too worried. I figured I'd get a contract eventually. They just came right out and said, "No. Dennis is probably going to play in the minors for two years. He needs to get a little stronger and work on certain things."

Boom Boom countered with, "No, no. My Dennis score you lots of goals. He no go minor. He play on this team right now." I was still laughing because of the way he was talking. I figured all I could do was go out and play. That night against L.A., I did. And I got myself a contract.

Boom Boom got me a three-year deal. It paid me $30,000 for my first year, $40,000 for my second year, and $50,000 for year number three. It also came with a $30,000 signing bonus. So that bar tab back in Salt Lake City wasn't the end of the world.

I was pumped. And to be honest, I didn't even care about the terms of the contract. All I wanted to do was play. Still, it was a lot of money at the time. I decided that I'd use a good chunk of the cash to say thanks to my mom and dad. I asked them, "What would you like?" They wanted a pool so they could entertain friends, so we installed one in their backyard, the same yard where my dad built that little rink 12 years earlier.

We had some great times at that pool. Mom and Dad were a pretty popular couple after it went in. And you never knew who'd drop by Chez Maruk. I remember lounging around the pool one summer, and my brother Kenny dropped by with a kid he had just met at an awards banquet at West Humber Collegiate High School. Maybe Kenny was trying to impress his new pal by showing him his parents' pool. Or maybe he was showing off his brother who had just wrapped up his first NHL season. My brother did the intros — he told me this guy was a big-time player. "Dennis, this is Wayne Gretzky," my brother said. I reached out and shook hands with the kid who would one day become the greatest to ever play the game. "I'll see you on the ice, kid," I said. I gave young 99 the big-league treatment the first time I ever met him. We'd have plenty more meetings in the years to come.

10 THIS IS THE NHL?

"I'm not the biggest guy out there, either. But you can't show any fear. Obviously, if you are counted on to score goals, you're going to have to work through punishment. I don't remember Dennis ever backing down from any confrontation; he always went into the dirty areas. Dennis, in his early years, had to stand up for himself because people would challenge him just to see what he was made of."
— Rick Middleton, 988 career NHL regular-season points

In the fall of 1975, I headed off to my new hockey home, Oakland, California. I was an NHLer, a California Seal. A quick refresher on the Seals — they were in Oakland for nine seasons. My first year in Oakland was the team's last. In 698 games, the Seals won a grand total of 182 games. The team was always in a state of flux — they might be moving across the bay, or they might be moving anywhere, or everywhere. We had some diehard fans, but not a lot of them. The year before I showed up, the Seals averaged 6,172 attendees per home game.

So I joined this bunch, armed with a new contract but essentially all alone. My fiancée, Joni, stayed back in London, Ontario. She was attending Western University and still had to finish her degree. As her education was winding down, mine was just beginning.

We started off the season with a trip to Atlanta. We walked away with a 4–3 win. The only reason I know that is from looking it up on the internet; I have no recollection of my first NHL game. That doesn't sound all that romantic, but I just really can't recall the game. I do know I didn't score a goal. I picked up my first NHL point in our next game. I got an assist on an Al MacAdam goal in a win over the Wings. But my lack of goal scoring continued. For the first time in my hockey career, I was in a goal-scoring slump. I finally managed to score my first NHL goal in the team's eighth game that season. And guess where we were? Yep, Toronto, of course. And on a Saturday night no less.

It's kind of weird, but I don't remember a lot of my goals — maybe I go into some strange goal-scoring zone where I lose my mind — but I do remember my first one. It was the first period and we were already up 1–0. We were short-handed, with Ralph Klassen in the box. I guess the team liked my speed because they had me killing penalties — and it worked. We were in the Leafs zone, I was in the slot, Mike Christie hit me with a pass, and I let one rip. I beat Wayne Thomas low on the glove-hand side. BOOM. It was 2–0 Seals. At the age of 19, I had my first NHL goal.

It was really special to score that goal at Maple Leaf Gardens. Not because I grew up cheering for the Leafs, and not because I had played in that rink for the Marlies. It was really special to score that goal at Maple Leaf Gardens because my mom and dad were there to see me score. Every time I played against the Leafs, it was always a huge family affair for all of the Maruks. Whenever my team would fly into Toronto, I'd skip the ride to our downtown hotel and just head right to my mom and dad's place. If I needed to go downtown to meet the team for a skate, I'd hop on a train and head down to the Gardens. I started that tradition my first year in the league and kept it going for pretty much my entire NHL career. It is a fact: no matter how tough and mean your favourite NHLer may look, he misses his parents. We'd have a big family dinner whenever I was in Toronto, hit up a restaurant or something, then I'd try to put on a little show on the ice. On October 25, 1975, I delivered with NHL goal number one. We tied the Leafs 2–2. We Seals were off to a pretty decent start: three wins, three losses, and two ties. But then it all fell apart.

Despite it all, from the very start of the season until the very end, I continued to practise what Dave Hutchison had preached to me: *be a prick.*

In my rookie season, I hacked and slashed and hit anything and everyone that I could. Even something as simple as a faceoff was a chance for me to establish myself and to let the other centre, and the entire opposing team for that matter, know that the little rubber puck belonged to me. I did whatever I had to to create space for myself. A few years into my career, I was taking a faceoff against that kid I had met at my parents' pool in 1976. I was playing my usual rough and, some would say, greasy game. Wayne and I were lining up for the draw. He just looked at me and said, "Why are you hitting and fighting?" I had a simple answer: "I'm not going to change the way I play. Are you going to change the way you play? Are you going to start fighting?" Wayne didn't say a word. They dropped the puck and on we went. I wasn't 99, I wasn't Bobby Orr, I wasn't Phil Esposito. I was me. And the only way I could survive in the NHL was by being a prick. If it pissed people off, so be it. A guy like me needed his space.

I like to think the head coach of the Seals, Jack Evans, agreed as well. I mean, why did he use *me* on the penalty kill? Well, maybe because with one less guy on the ice he figured there was more space for a smaller and creative player like me. That shorty against the Leafs for my first NHL goal was one of five short-handed goals I scored that season — a record for an NHL rookie.

Once my initial seven-game scoring slump came to an end, the pucks started to go in on a more regular basis. On November 18, 1975, it seemed like I was skating for the Knights again. I scored four goals in a 5–3 win over the Pittsburgh Penguins. Al MacAdam assisted on three of them, which was a sign of things to come; Al and I were a pretty decent duo for a few seasons. By this night in November, though, I was at seven goals on the season. It was early, but Rookie of the Year talk was already out there, as you can tell from an Associated Press article on my four-goal night. I told them:

> "I decided not to think about Rookie of the Year until I got my first hat trick. The last couple of games we had not been skating well and I was thinking more of helping the team. We know we can skate with any line in the league."

Trying to keep the puck from future Hall of Famer Bobby Clarke during my rookie year with the Seals.

We did, for a little bit, but we were anything but a threat to win the Stanley Cup. It was a long season, but I was pleased with how I fared as a rookie. We won our final game of the year 5–2 in front of 6,442 loud Seals fans. I scored two goals and was greeted by their now more than familiar chants of "Maruuuuk, Maruuuuk!" But we were not going to the playoffs, and that was a bummer. I had proved to myself, however, that I belonged in the NHL. The following Monday in the *San Mateo County Times*, one of the headlines read, "Flying Finish for Seals Rookie." The article, written by Dick Draper — how great is that name for a hockey writer? It's almost just like Dickie Dunn in *Slapshot* — stated that when I showed up at camp, I was a "*pipsqueakish imp.*"

Draper's words, not mine. He went on to say:

> *But there was no doubting his I-shall-never-tarry traits, and teammates were quick to learn that this small package of puckish protoplasm was to be reckoned with.*

> *It didn't take long for the rest of the league to find out, either. Maruk was a diminutive dynamo during his rookie year.*

Well, thanks Dick. I set a club record for goals and assists by a rookie — 30 and 32, respectively — and points by a rookie. I also set an NHL rookie record with five short-handed goals. The team's booster club voted me the Seals' Most Popular Player. Despite our team's record of 27-42-11 and our dead-last finish in the Adams Division, our future looked bright. I told my buddy Dick Draper:

> *"It was a great year, something I just didn't expect.*

> *"We're not pushovers anymore. Next year, teams will be thinking about us. We've got some tough guys on our team and we'll be a lot better and a lot stronger.*

> *"I know I will. I've got that year under my belt, and I know I can score goals now in the NHL."*

11 NO, THIS IS THE NHL?

"It's a big step from junior to the pros, and he came right in. He was just a little green on the side, so I took him under my wing. I did that with most of the kids. Dennis was pretty receptive. He was a free, happy-going guy, so it was an easy transition for him."

— Gilles Meloche, Seals goaltender

Now I should tell you about life off the ice as an NHL rookie. The first thing I had to do when I moved to Oakland was find a place to live. A bunch of my teammates lived in a condo complex about 20 minutes away from our arena. That seemed like a good fit. My teammate Bob Girard and I decided to get a place together. He was a little older than me, but he was an NHL rookie as well. Being around the boys really helped me settle into a place that was so far away from home — remember, I was still a teenager.

Our goalie Gilles Meloche lived in the same complex. He and his late wife Nicole, who was just a super lady, were beyond kind to me. Nicole and Gilles would invite Bob and me over to their place for dinner. They'd make nice home-cooked meals for us and make us feel right at home. It was quite a scene. Gilles was French, Nicole was French, Bob was French, and I was some dumb Ukrainian kid from Toronto.

They introduced me to the finer things in life, like Mateus Rose wine. My Rexdale lemon gin days were way behind me. I remember sipping something much lighter and looking at the Mateus. Gilles said, "Get rid of that grape juice. Here's some real good stuff." It was definitely an acquired taste, and the Meloches did their best to help me acquire it.

After finding a place to live, I did what any young "rich" athlete did in the mid-1970s: I bought a sports car. Back in London, I used to get around in a '66 Beaumont. Well, those days were over. I bought a 1973 Corvette — a sweet ride. The '73 was the last year they had the T-chrome on the back. I thought the NHL was about scoring goals and winning games; turns out, there was much more to it.

I was convinced that once the season started, the partying would settle down. At training camp, we would head to practice and then head to the bar. In the regular season, we would play a game and then head to the bar. And when we didn't have a game — boom, meet at the bar. Go for lunch, have a few. "It's lunch, gotta meet at the bar. It's a team thing, we gotta bond as a team." Now, you didn't have to drink, but pretty much everyone did. Very few guys said no. I soon discovered that day-to-day life in the NHL consisted of one party after another.

And we didn't drink alone. The California Seals were a very hospitable bunch. After all, our visitors had travelled across the

In tight to the net against the St. Louis Blues. I scored 30 goals during my first NHL season. The goal total was good enough for a bonus that I didn't get.

Credit: Portnoy/Hockey Hall of Fame

continent to come and play against us, so why not invite them out. Yep, the Seals and, let's say, the New York Rangers would go at it toe to toe all night long in a hack and slash, punch you in the face mid-'70s hockey game, and then we'd go out and tip back a few after the final buzzer.

Of course, when you're burning the candle at both ends like most players did in the '70s, you may hurt the next day, which was what the morning skate was for. Burn off the booze with some exercise and then get a little fresher with an afternoon nap. That regimen, however, didn't always get everything out of the system, and there was the odd time when the previous night's festivities would hang with you the next day, but no matter how bad you felt, you still had a job to do.

On more than one occasion, I remember banging into a guy along the boards during a game, only to be greeted by an elbow and the smell of booze. I saw some guys pound back a few on game day, you know, the old liquid lunch. After tipping back a few with your burger, it was time for a quick power nap and then on to the rink for the game. Man, it sure was different back then. I would love to see the faces on some of today's players if they saw our "nutrition" plan.

I always tried to be respectful of the game, though. I was not a liquid lunch guy. I had a good time, I know that, but I tried to get my rest and play the game. If my opponents were a little off their game, that wasn't my fault. I wanted to be the best every time I stepped out onto the ice.

Pro hockey players sure liked having fun, though.

12 VETERAN ADVICE

"My folks kind of threatened me, 'You get your degree or else!' I commuted back and forth a little bit. I really wanted to finish up my schooling, and I was glad I did in the long run."

— Joni

At one of our soirees with a visiting team one night at the Oakland-Alemidian, I happened to come across one of the most flamboyant playboys in the NHL. I'd watched this guy on the ice for years; he was a fantastic hockey player. He looked over at me and said, "Dennis, you're a good hockey player." I said thank you very much. Then he said, "No, you're a great hockey player." I was flattered — this was high praise coming from a player who I respected and admired.

So the two of us began talking. I remember he was sitting on a ledge in this giant condo, taking it all in, surveying the entire room. The conversation quickly went from life on the ice to life off the ice. "Are you engaged?" he asked. I told him yes, I was a committed man who was going to get married. He was not impressed. "What are you doing that for?"

I was stumped. "What do you mean? I love the girl and she loves me. And we're going to start a great life ..." Now, I wasn't stupid. I saw what went on with some of the guys on the team and other guys in the league. I wanted to get married because I was in love and I wanted to start a family. I didn't want to be *one of those guys*.

My newfound friend took a moment to ponder my answer. To review: I was a hockey player, I was committed to one woman, and I didn't want to have a *girlfriend* on the side. My friend looked over at me. He had found his answer to my "problem." "Just get a hooker. You know, call her anything you want. You pay your first couple of times and the next thing you know, she won't take your money — if she likes you. You don't have to get married ... why get married ... we all have problems."

Here I was, an impressionable 19-year-old, trying to figure out how to survive in the world of professional hockey, and this was the advice I was getting from one of the stars of the game. I didn't know everything when I was 19, but I knew enough to take a pass on those words of wisdom.

13 YOU STILL OWE ME!

"I never heard this story. That surprises me — I never had any problem while I was there because all the contracts were backed up by the league."

— Gilles Meloche

I headed back home to Toronto in the spring of 1976 as a bona fide NHLer. I had the car, the hair, the clothes, the fiancée, and the cash. Wait — I had most of my cash. But not all of it.

I had done my part on the ice, 30 goals and 32 assists in my rookie year. Remember, the Seals brass had told Boom Boom that their initial plan for me was to spend a year in the minors. I didn't need that. I proved it in camp and I delivered when the puck dropped for real.

Now, old Boom Boom was more than confident in me, and he got a few bonus clauses sewn into my contract. Thanks to my on-ice performance in my rookie season, I racked up a cool $15,000 in bonuses. What a way to kick off the summer. There was just one problem: the lawyers that Boom Boom worked for out of Montreal did not have a copy of this clause in my contract, and Boom Boom also didn't have a copy of the clause. I sure as hell didn't have a copy of the clause; that's what I paid these guys for. I was told that the bonus clause was on a separate sheet of paper, and they had lost it.

To make matters worse, the Seals weren't playing ball at all. Why? Because they had no money. Or, at least, that's what they were saying. When you average just over 5,600 fans during your nine years in the league, you are not exactly counting your fortune. Add to the fact that we had just missed the playoffs for the sixth year in a row, and you've got yourself a few problems.

My problem was the Seals did not want to pay me my $15,000. Their stance was essentially that if I wanted my bonus money, I had to prove that it was a clause in my contract. My lawyers did not have a copy of the clause, so I was out of luck. The team was not about to hand over a copy of the contract in an act of good faith, so I was screwed. I did what any other hockey player would have done at the time: I called the Eagle.

You've all heard the stories, and depending on how you look at it, he was either a saviour or pariah. But in the 1970s, if you had a problem, you called Alan Eagleson. It wasn't until years later that we learned what was really going on.

I had never met Eagleson until this point in my life. I didn't think the bonus clause mix-up was Boom Boom's fault, but I had to do something. I remember introducing myself to Eagleson. He knew who I was. I essentially told him my problem: "The Seals owe me a $15,000 bonus, but my lawyers don't have a copy of the bonus clause. The Seals won't pay me if we can't prove that bonus exists." Eagleson didn't take too long to come to a conclusion: if my lawyers couldn't prove that the clause exists, I was out $15,000. There was nothing I could do. That shows you how "powerful" the Players' Association was back in the day. We just had to take the Seals at their word. If they said the clause didn't exist, then the clause didn't exist. I started that off-season $15,000 in the hole.

And that's also how I started my relationship with Alan Eagleson. This may shock some of you, but I still consider him a friend. Alan Eagleson stayed with me for the rest of my career. He was my agent right up until I played my final game in the National Hockey League in 1989.

I will say this about Alan: he never did anything wrong to me. He just managed my contracts; he never handled my money. When it was time to hammer out a new deal, Eagleson took care of it and that was it. I know what happened with Bobby Orr and I know what happened with the PA. He helped to start the Players' Association, ran the thing for close to 20 years, and was convicted of fraud in Canada and the USA for embezzling money. Eagleson did time behind bars. A lot of guys from my era can't stand him. They won't even shake his hand, but I'm not one of them. I think that says more about me than it does about him. I'm just not wired that way.

When he was in trouble with the law, I remember telling him that I really didn't want to talk to him about it or know about all the problems he was having. As far as I was concerned, that was between him and the other guys; it had nothing to do with me. I just said to him, "I don't want to talk about it. You'll always be my friend, and I respect what you did for me and my career."

In fact, when my mom died, Eagleson showed up at the funeral. That is something I will never forget. If I bumped into him today, I'd be more than happy to sit down and have a coffee and a chat with him. What he did with the players' money was wrong. There is no doubt about that. But I'm not one to hold a grudge. I hear the Eagle and his wife, Nancy, are big tennis buffs now, and he is into flipping real estate. I wish he could have figured out a way to get the Seals to flip me that $15,000 in bonus money. No matter, I had other things on my mind in the summer of 1976.

14 HELLO, CLEVELAND

"What was Richfield Coliseum like? It was like looking at ushers. All you saw were ushers because there was nobody else in the building."

— Rick Hampton

Joni and I got married in the summer of 1976. It was a great time. A bunch of my teammates from the Seals made it to the wedding.

Starting a marriage is never easy. It is even more difficult when you don't know where you are going to live. That entire off-season, the Seals' owners had been contemplating the future of the team. I was cool with Oakland; the owners, however, were not. Was the team going to move to Denver? Or were we going to Cleveland or Buffalo? I decided to do what most hockey players would do: I didn't really worry about it and enjoyed my summer.

And then, finally, the phone rang. It was like draft day all over again. On the other end of the line was a man who was telling me where I was going to live and where I was going to play.

Good-bye California sunshine and hello . . . Cleveland. That's right, Cleveland. The Seals' owner, Mel Swig, had big plans for the team, but they never materialized. Swig had wanted to build an arena in San Francisco. Not everyone shared those plans, though, and once Swig's dreams of a San Francisco arena were crushed, so were the Seals. The city voted against the proposal. The Seals were leaving. One of the Seals' part-owners, George Gund, was from Cleveland, so I guess that clinched the deal. And just like that, my days as a Seal were over, and instead of heading to a city on the Bay, my new bride and I were going to a city on Lake Erie!

A year earlier, I had to do my research on Oakland. Now, it was time to do some research on Cleveland. The city was in Ohio, they had a basketball team, and they used to have a WHA team. And with that knowledge, we were headed off to Cleveland, or should I say, the Cleveland area.

The all-new Cleveland Barons decided to play out of the Richfield Coliseum, in the middle of nowhere. The Coliseum was located about 20 miles outside of the city proper. It was basically halfway between Cleveland and Akron in the middle of, well, a field. The plan was to draw fans to the Coliseum from both cities — that plan did not work. Fans failed to show up, in record numbers. The Richfield Coliseum was a massive building; it seated over 18,000 for hockey games and it was cavernous. It looked even bigger when only 4,000 people were in the stands.

We drove down to Cleveland and looked for a place to live. Just like in Oakland, a bunch of players moved into the same complex, this time in Akron. It was called Timberland Park. Some of the older guys on the team bought houses, but a lot of us lived in Timberland Park. Ralph Klassen, set up shop there and we became really good friends. I was the emcee at his wedding in Saskatoon. I haven't seen Ralph in years, but we were tight when we were Barons. As players, we bonded closely in Cleveland, likely because we went through a lot of negative stuff both on and off the ice.

For example, on opening night, over half the seats were empty. Only 8,899 fans showed up to watch us skate to a 2–2 tie against the L.A. Kings. Three nights later, it was worse: 5,209 fans watched us beat the Washington Capitals. I scored a goal in both games. It's just too bad hardly anyone noticed. I've been asked if it was tough to play in front of such small crowds. I always answer, "It was my job." You can't worry about how many people are in the stands, you just have to go out and play. Hopefully, you win a few games and the seats start to fill up. I didn't look at the attendance problems in Cleveland and think it was my job to fill the seats. I thought it was my job to win hockey games and beat the top teams in the league. That would be my contribution to drawing the fans.

Our coach Jack Evans put me on a line with Al MacAdam and Bob Murdoch. We clicked. We were called "the 3M Line," and as we went, so went the Barons. We were a streaky team; we'd win a few, then lose a few, and sometimes a few more. Right before Christmas of 1976, we strung together five wins in seven games. Then we racked up six straight losses; we were drawing flies. On January 5, 1977, 4,166 fans showed up to watch us in a 3–2 loss to the Boston Bruins. If you can't draw a crowd when the big bad Bruins come to town, you are in trouble.

We were in big, bad trouble . . .

15 HOT NEWS

I tried to help the Barons' cause as best I could. I mentioned earlier that it wasn't my job to put butts in the seats, but I felt the need to help out. I decided to try to raise some cash for the penniless Barons; I became a pencil salesman. Man, we used to have a ton of fun in the airports back in those days. Remember, this was back before teams flew on charters. We flew with everybody else, and we would have some really long road trips and a lot of time to kill, so to pass the time I liked to give the guys an odd chuckle or two. I put a bunch of pencils in a coffee cup and I would sell them for a nickel or 10 cents each at our gate in the airport.

One of the things we thought was wildly entertaining was "Hot News." Airport security in the late '70s was, shall we say, very casual. You could do pretty much whatever you wanted back then, especially if you were a pro hockey player. Lighting fires in an airport terminal, for example. When one of our teammates was trying to educate himself by reading a newspaper, we'd quickly put an end to that. Someone would get out a lighter and sneak under his seat. In the meantime, one of my teammates or I would go over to the guy reading the paper and start some small chitchat: "Look at that pretty woman over there. She's hot, isn't she?" Once operation distraction was in full force, my cohort under the chair would light the corner of the paper, and then, *boom*, the guy is holding a flaming newspaper. He would immediately jump out of his chair, throw the paper onto the floor, and stomp out the fire. It was hilarious. People would be looking around at this collection of 20-something long-haired hockey players in stitches and wonder what in the hell was going on. Security never said a thing. No one ever said a thing, except us. And you could never understand what we were saying through our fits of laughter. And if you were wondering where a group of elite athletes would get a lighter from — that's easy. About half the team smoked back then. Darts were in fashion right up until the early '80s.

Different cities would lend themselves to different gags. Whenever we'd visit Boston, one of the guys would buy a lobster, tie a string on it, and walk it around the airport. Again, we thought this was hilarious. Other travellers, maybe less so, but we'd always try to let them in on our gags.

If one of the guys on our team was from the Boston area, he usually paid the price on our flight out of town as well. Chances are he'd have to buy a bunch of tickets for family and friends to go to the game, and he'd likely stay out late with his buddies. That meant that on the flight he would usually try to take a nap. As soon as he would fall asleep, we'd grab a lobster or two and place on the guy's chest. He'd eventually wake up, and there was always a scream. I remember we did it to Mike Fidler, a young guy out of Boston, and we got him good. We put the lobster on him, he woke up, and his eyes grew huge. He grabbed the lobster and threw it. The flying lobster hit another passenger across the aisle. Once again, hilarity ensued. The pilot would likely turn the plane around if something like that happened these days. We were civil about the whole thing, though. We kept the elastic bands on the lobster's claws so they wouldn't pinch anyone . . . safety first, right?

These days, can you imagine what the fine would be for a player who missed a flight? I can't. Well, how about a coach missing a flight? Not too long after the financial follies of the Cleveland Barons became too much, I was with my new team in Washington. The Caps were a hurting bunch during Dan Belisle's 90-game tenure as the team's head coach. Under Dan's leadership in the late 1970s, the Caps managed to win just 28 of 90. Dan had a problem with the players — and that problem was nobody liked him.

Dan showed up at the airport for one flight in less-than-ideal travelling condition. He sat down across from me with a black eye. I took another look and his tie was on crooked and his jacket was kind of hanging off him. Dan was half in the bag. He said he had fallen and hit his head on a coffee table. Before we knew it, Dan had passed out or nodded off to sleep, depending on how you look at it. Each one of the Washington Capitals quietly walked past their coach and onto the flight. We got on the plane and no one said a word. The flight attendants did their usual thing, running us through a safety check. There was still no sign of our coach. The captain told the flight attendants to prepare for takeoff. There was still no sign of Dan. We started to pull out of our gate. Still no coach. We raced down the runway and into the skies — Dan Belisle, the head coach of the Washington Capitals, was still asleep at the gate. He missed our flight and, man, did we laugh. He must have caught the next flight because he did make it to our game on time.

We always had a blast. You had to in those days, whether it was with the Caps, where I did get paid, or in Cleveland, where I didn't. It all came to a head one night in February 1977. We had a game to play against the Sabres, but as far as we knew, our season was over.

16 LIQUID LUNCH AND A HOCKEY GAME

"I think we thought it was over and we were wondering
how we were going to get paid and stuff like that."

— Rick Hampton

One of the great things about being a professional hockey player is you get paid to play the game you love. Unless you were on the Cleveland Barons in February 1977. Our owner was losing millions of dollars; he was losing so much money he couldn't pay his players. This, of course, was a problem. We couldn't win and no one was watching our games. And now no one was paying us to play them.

Mr. Swig was meeting with the NHL, trying to scrounge up the cash to keep the team on the go. A team in financial trouble was nothing out of the ordinary in the mid- to late-1970s. Several WHA teams folded, but this wasn't supposed to happen in the NHL. We didn't get paid on February 1, 1977. We were told we'd get our cheques later that month. It's tough to play

A bearded Baron. It could get lonely in the cavernous Richfield Coliseum.

when you're not getting paid and you don't know how long your team is going to be around for.

On February 23, 1977, we hit the ice for our morning skate, and then word spread fast: the team was going to fold and there would be a dispersal draft, sending us to different teams around the league. The team didn't have enough money to cover our paycheques — there wasn't even enough money to cover our insurance. The Barons were toast. Upon hearing this news, we did what any group of young, finely tuned professional athletes would do — we hit the bar.

We got together as a team for our last supper — or lunch — and a few pops. I think we were at a place called the Nightclub

Peninsula. It was where our fans would hang out, not too far from the Coliseum. We showed up around noon and had a bite to eat, then a few wobbly pops. We were having a good time, a few laughs, and saying our goodbyes. Who knew where in the hell we would end up? We just knew that we were no longer going to be in Cleveland.

It ended up being a pretty long lunch. At around 4:30, our team's player rep, Bob Stewart, was summoned to the bar. He had a phone call. Someone on the other end of the line told him that there had been a last-minute reprieve. Bobby came back and told us the news: "We have a game. Go home, change, and head to the Coliseum." Our cash had been covered and the Barons were still alive. Now, keep in mind, we'd been having a few and game time was a little over two hours away.

But it wasn't exactly a mad rush to get out of the Peninsula. I'm pretty sure I finished my drink, and I know a few of the other guys did as well. I eventually got home, freshened up, changed my clothes, and headed for the rink. A bunch of suits at a much higher pay grade than us had put a plan in place that kept the Barons in business. But we were still the Barons. The Sabres beat us 5–3 with just over 3,000 fans in the stands. After the loss, our record stood at 18 wins, 32 losses, and 10 ties. We had 20 games to go.

We were a team struggling on the ice, struggling at the gate, struggling at the bank, and struggling for publicity. You had to wonder if anyone in Cleveland, aside from the 5,000 and change in the stands, knew we were even there. With loss after loss, even the newspapers were looking for any new angle. "Barons' Beards Counter Hockey's Clean Cut Image" was the headline on a story in the *Chronicle Telegram* on March 10, 1977. Any publicity is good publicity, I guess. "It's a matter of being ourselves," my teammate Len Frig said in the story. "We're playing for personal pride now. Before, we weren't playing that well and were uptight. Now, we're loose."

We were loose enough to finish the season with one win in our last seven games, and I led the Barons in scoring with 28 goals, 50 assists, and 78 points in 80 games. But for the second time in my two NHL seasons, my team was not going to the playoffs. Unfortunately, this was something I was going to have to get used to — teams that couldn't cut it on or off the ice.

17 NOBODY DREAMS OF THE BARONS

"Some of the teams Dennis played on weren't the best, but because he was on the team you couldn't just think that you had the two points in the bag. He could make a lot of things happen, and he got a lot of ice time and a lot of power plays . . . he was one of the guys you had to watch, and it wasn't easy."

— Rick Middleton

When I was a kid, I dreamed of playing for the Toronto Maple Leafs or the Montreal Canadiens. I certainly never dreamed of playing for the Cleveland Barons — of course, when I was a kid, there were no Cleveland Barons. But here I was, in my third year in the NHL, as a Cleveland Baron for the second year in a row. The question was, did anybody care? It was kind of a pointless question. If no one watched, there wasn't much I could do about it. And the reality of the situation was, when you were a Cleveland Baron, no one watched.

A little over ten thousand fans showed up for our home opener on October 15, 1977. By Cleveland standards, it was a huge crowd. But in the massive cave that was the Richfield Coliseum, the empty seats almost outnumbered the ones with butts in them.

Attendance was likely a reflection of the fact that we played miles outside of Cleveland. And we were not exactly tearing it up on the ice. Case in point, in early December, we lost a game by 10 goals. Yes, *10*. The Flyers beat us 11–1 in Philly. I broke Bernie Parent's shutout attempt with 65 seconds to go. We Barons were part of NHL history that night. Flyers defenceman Tom Bladon set an NHL record for most points by a defenceman in a game. He had four goals and four assists in the Philly win, and our coach Jack Evans summed things up best after the game: "No comment," he said. "What can you say about a game like this?"

Again, I was asking myself, *Is this really the NHL?* Well, it was, and it was really made clear when we visited places like Montreal, where the game was almost a religion. If the Barons were a forgotten bunch in Cleveland, the Habs were revered and worshipped in Montreal.

When we played the Canadiens, I was often on the ice against Guy Lafleur. There's a great picture of me chasing Guy around the back of the net at the Forum. Man, he could fly. In my rookie year with the Seals, the Habs beat us 1–0 in Montreal. Clarence Campbell, the president of the league, came into our dressing room after the game and told us it was one of the best games he had ever seen. Lafleur had the only goal of the game that night. He whacked in a rebound to give the Habs the win.

When I was in my early twenties, it was almost a surreal feeling to be playing against a guy like Lafleur. But at least he reminded me, through his play, that I was in the NHL. I was playing against the best in the world. It was amazing to watch Guy because he was so good with the puck and he was so fast. I heard he smoked two packs a day. My teammates and I always wondered how a guy could smoke so much and perform like that.

The thing about Lafleur is people never really compare him to anybody. When people talk about the best players to ever play the game, it is always: Howe, Gretzky, Orr, Lemieux. You never hear anyone say Guy Lafleur is the best. But I honestly think he was one of the best forwards to ever play the game. I think Guy is often dismissed because the teams he played on in Montreal were so good. Well, Gretzky played on some very good teams in Edmonton, too.

Another guy I loved to line up against was Phil Esposito. You could not move Phil. Playing against him brought out the best in me. It was a thrill and a challenge to play against one of the best goal scorers of all time. One night, we were playing the Rangers and were up 3–2; I had scored all three goals for us. With about a minute left in the game, I had a faceoff against Esposito at centre ice. I wanted a fourth goal. I predicted that Phil would try to push the puck between my legs and then go forward and dump it in. I let him win the faceoff but then stopped the puck with my skate. Phil took off thinking the puck had slipped between my legs, and I took it up the ice and scored. It was an honour to play against a guy like Phil Esposito. There were some frustrating times during my first few years in the

NHL, but there were some great moments as well.

The Barons made a few trades at the beginning of 1978. We picked up some solid veterans, guys like J.P. Parise and Jean Potvin. The next thing you knew, we knocked off one of the most powerful teams in the league. In front of a nowhere-near capacity crowd of 2,074 — yes, you read that right — we beat the New York Islanders 5–3. I scored a shortie in the second, my 24th goal of the year, to give us a 3–2 lead. I finished with three points, and that win was the first of three wins in a row.

Then came February and March of 1978. We may have had a few new faces, but we were the same old Barons. We went 15 games in a row without a win. We had five ties in those 15 games. We finally broke that streak on March 29. It was a 7–3 win over the Minnesota North Stars. I scored my 31st of the season. Gilles Meloche got the win. As per usual, he was a very busy man. He made 32 saves.

Poor Gilles. My buddy from my rookie year in California was still with us. He might have been the busiest man in the National Hockey League in the mid- to late-'70s. He was a great goalie on some very bad teams. Gilles has been vastly underrated as a goalie. Like me, he never really had a chance to play on a good team — but that doesn't mean he wasn't a good goalie. Here was a guy who knew he was going to face a ton of shots every night and was always up to the task. Gilles Meloche was one tough guy to score on — I know, I practised against the guy for years. We ended up playing together in Oakland, Cleveland, and Minnesota.

The Barons had five more games to go after that win against the North Stars. We won two, lost two, and tied one. We lost our final game of the year 3–2 to the Pittsburgh Penguins, and 7,364 fans were there to see it. My second goal of the night was my 36th goal of the season and the last in the history of the Cleveland Barons.

18 MINNESOTA OR BUST — I'LL TAKE BUST

"It was kind of a nightmare from our perspective. We had heard rumblings. When you merge two teams like that, with Cleveland going into Minnesota, there were going to be trades."

— Joni

We won 22 games during my second year in Cleveland and missed the playoffs. It didn't take a genius to figure out that the future of the NHL in Cleveland was bleak.

Cleveland wasn't the only NHL team struggling at the gate and on the ice. The Minnesota North Stars won only 18 games in 1977–78, one more than the Washington Capitals, who finished dead last in the league that season. Before I knew it, I'd be wearing the colours of both of those franchises.

Just like Cleveland, the North Stars drew flies in 1977–78. Their average crowd was 8,666 that year — the lowest in team history. The Barons were in trouble. The North Stars were in trouble. The NHL came up with a solution: get rid of the Barons and merge them with the Stars. In the summer of 1978, the Barons and Stars became one, and NHL hockey in Cleveland was dead. I was now a Minnesota North Star — but not for long.

Lou Nanne was the general manager of the Minnesota North Stars. Like any GM, he had his guys. Guys he drafted and brought up in the organization. Guys he had faith in. Despite the fact that I scored a career-high 36 goals in 1977–78, I was not one of Nanne's guys. Lou made this very clear when I showed up in Minnesota. He told me, "I'm going to keep my centremen." Of course, this was a problem for me because I was a centreman. Nanne had drafted the high-scoring Bobby Smith first overall in the 1978 draft. Smith scored 192 points with the Ottawa 67's the previous year. When you draft a kid like that first overall, he definitely figures into your plans. Smith fit, and, according to Nanne, I did not.

To his credit, Nanne was up front. That summer, he told me he was going to trade me for a first-round pick. I figured there was no sense in going to Minnesota if I was going to be traded, so that summer I waited around for a deal. Well, summer turned into early September and I was still a North Star.

The next thing I know, Lou is on the phone, asking me to come to Minnesota for training camp. "You'll love it here. The fans are going to love you," he said, but my agent, Alan Eagleson, told me that something was coming down the pipe. "Don't buy a house," he told me. I'm glad I listened to that advice.

I got to Minnesota and rented a house in Bloomington, not far from where we played at the Met Center, but there was a problem: I wasn't playing. Our coach Harry Howell sat me on the bench for the first two games of the season; I think I may have gotten in one shift. I knew something was happening. I went to Harry and said, "Come on, Harry. I talked to my agent — I know something is up. Can't you just tell me?" He said he couldn't play me because if I got injured, Minnesota couldn't trade me.

Our third game of the season was against the Vancouver Canucks. It was a 7 o'clock game. I was getting set to go to the game when the phone rang at around 4:30. It was Max McNab, the general manager of the Washington Capitals. He told me he had just traded a first-round pick for me. I was now a Washington Capital. This was interesting.

19 HELLO, GOODBYE

*"The night that I got there, they traded him. I was left
in a city that I had no idea about. I hadn't met anybody.
Typically, the players' wives really help each other in a trade
situation but I didn't know anybody. Dennis had to fly out
the next day. I can remember the GM of Washington calling
me and welcoming me to Washington, and I believe I burst
into tears."*

— Joni

Within five minutes, Lou Nanne called me. "We just traded you
to Washington."

"I already know. Thanks a lot," I said. I told Lou I was going
to head down to the rink to pick up a few things — after all, I
already had my suit on.

Very shortly after that, my wife and her sister pulled up to the
house. I had arrived in Minnesota a few weeks before, while Joni
and her sister got ready for the move. They drove our two cars all
the way to Minnesota from Cleveland. My wife pulled into the

driveway, excited and ready to start her new life. I greeted her with "I just got traded." She couldn't believe it — she was pretty upset, to say the least.

Then, to make matters worse, J.P. Parise and Bryan Maxwell pulled up to my house. They were my ride to the game. I walked out to them and said, "Good luck in your game tonight."

"What do you mean?"

"I just got traded," I said. I was known as a prankster back in the day, and they thought this was another one of my jokes. "Come on, you're kidding."

They opened the back door to the car and started nudging away. "Get in," they told me. "We're going."

"No, I've been traded," I told them again. "I'm going to Washington for a first-round pick."

I went back into the house and talked to Joni. Thankfully, Max McNab called again and told us the Capitals would take care of our cars, so at least Joni wouldn't have another massive drive in front of her. The Caps even said they would fly Joni to Washington whenever she was ready to make the move. I, of course, had to fly to D.C. right away. Being the wife of a hockey player is not easy. Max McNab was really nice about the whole situation. He even made sure he talked to Joni on the phone. "You're going to love Washington," he told her. Once that call was finished and everything was settled, or as settled as it could be, I headed down to the rink to pick up my stuff.

It was not a pretty night at the Met Center, for a variety of reasons. The North Stars and Vancouver Canucks got into a big brawl. Curt Fraser clawed Bobby Smith's eyes in a fight. Poor Bobby wasn't a fighter, but Curt was. The brawl happened in the

With my first wife, Joni, who realized just how difficult it was to be a hockey player's wife.

third. After the game, I went into the dressing room because I wanted to say goodbye to the guys, some of whom I'd played with since I was a rookie in Oakland.

I was in the medical room with Bobby when Lou Nanne walked in. He came over and wanted to shake my hand. Now, remember, I had been told that I was going to be traded, then I was told to come to Minnesota, then I sat on the bench for two games, and then I was traded just as my wife showed up in Minnesota. I was not at all pleased to see him. I said, "I ain't shaking your hand. You're a liar. You lied to me, and you ruined my life. But I'm going to make it better."

Lou was just as fired up as I was. His best player just about had his eyes gouged out of his head, and now the guy he traded earlier in the day was letting him have it. For a second, I thought we were going to start throwing punches. Lou used to be a player, and he could hold his own. He didn't like what I had said to him, but he just walked away. We never shook hands that night.

We mended fences down the road, but in the heat of the moment, we were both frustrated. I was disappointed with how Lou and the North Stars had handled my situation. I said goodbye to the guys, and I was on my way to Washington the next morning.

20 CAPITAL CITY

If you think I was pumped to be traded to the Washington Capitals, you're dead wrong. The Caps had been a doormat since they entered the NHL a few years earlier, and the team had the fewest wins in the NHL the previous season.

I was on the move to yet another team struggling to stay afloat, and I kept asking myself: Why am I in this situation? Is this what my career is meant to be, playing for teams that can't win in front of empty seats night after night? Why am I always moving? Why can't I just be a Maple Leaf? That was my childhood dream — not this. Not life as a hockey vagabond. This was supposed to be the NHL.

I decided not to dwell on it for too long. I told myself that something good would happen, and things would change. I just had to keep playing hard and things would turn around and get better for me and my team. I couldn't play on last-place teams forever. I'd stop moving around every couple of years, and I would play for a franchise that was stable both on and off the ice. No more rallies to save teams. No more playing in front of

I found a home in Washington. I scored 431 points in 343 regular-season games with the Caps. Those 431 points are still in the Caps all-time top ten points leaders.

thousands of empty seats. I had to keep believing that things would change.

My first game with the Caps was in Landover, Maryland. We played in the outskirts of D.C. I didn't know it at the time, but on October 20, 1978, I played my first game in a place that would become my hockey home. I picked up my first point as a

Washington Capital when I assisted on a second period goal by Tom Rowe. It tied the game at two. We ended up losing to the Pittsburgh Penguins in front of 8,363 fans. Again I was playing in front of a sparse crowd for a struggling club, but I was determined to turn my career around with the Caps.

It just didn't happen right away. When I showed up in D.C. I didn't know any of my teammates. As I got to know them, things got better. When Joni and I bought a house, things got better. Just like in Oakland and in Cleveland, we lived in an area with a bunch of my teammates.

The Washington Capitals did not tear up the NHL in 1978–79, but I tried to stay positive. Tom Rowe and I were gelling on the ice, and it all culminated on the night of March 10, 1979, when everything we did seemed to work. Tom scored three goals in the first period and I assisted on all three as we stormed out to a 3–0 lead. Just under eight minutes into the second, Tom and I assisted on Gord Lane's first of the season to give us a 4–0 lead. Before the second period was over, we were up 6–2 on the St. Louis Blues, and I had a goal and four assists. I scored one more in the third. We beat the Blues 7–5. I set a Caps record with six points in one game.

My first season in Washington ended the same way my previous NHL seasons had ended — out of the playoffs. This was getting old. I had the most productive season of my career with 90 points, but I wanted some playoff hockey.

This is what I told the *Washington Post* in an article by Robert Fachet, published on April 7, 1979:

"My big goal was the playoffs. I thought we had a good chance, but with the injuries and the new players, it doesn't come overnight. I don't set any goals for myself, like 25 or 30 goals or 100 points or anything like that. I wanted to be in the playoffs and that will have to wait."

21 MR. INTERNATIONAL

"The big ice didn't matter that much because at the end of the day Dennis's game was within 30 feet of the net, and so, eventually, you had to get there. He could still play where he needed to play. You could play on Lake Ontario and you still have to get to the front of the net to score goals."

— Mike Gartner, Washington and Team Canada teammate

I figured if I couldn't get a taste of playoff hockey in the NHL, I could still find a way to play some meaningful games at the end of the NHL regular season. In 1979, for the second* spring in a row, I pulled on a Team Canada jersey and headed off to the World Hockey Championship.

The World Championship became my playoffs. I was there a lot — four* times in fact: 78, 79, 81, and 83. As of this writing, I'm 10th on Canada's all-time games played list at the Worlds with 35 appearances, and sixth all-time with 16 goals. I absolutely loved playing at the World Championship; the big ice had a lot to do with that.

The Worlds became my Stanley Cup playoffs. In Oakland and Cleveland and in my early days in Washington, we'd be out of the playoff race by Christmas. Luckily for me, I had something to look forward to in the spring.

I recently ran into Peter Stastny at a Hockey Hall of Fame event. We were on the ice for an alumni game, and we started chatting. Now, remember, before Peter and his brothers defected to Canada, they were huge stars with the Czechoslovakian national team. Peter and I started reminiscing, and memories of my almost annual European adventures came flooding back to both of us. "I remember you had all these goals," he told me. "Seven, eight goals. We had to stop you. You were a great scorer." He kept going on and on. It was awfully special to have a great Hall of Famer like Peter Stastny telling me all those things. I guess I made an impression on the Europeans. I keep hearing things like that more and more as the years go by. It's nice to know that I earned some respect both in the NHL and a long way from home over in Europe.

When I started going to the Worlds in 1978,* we would line up against the best the Soviets and the Eastern Bloc countries had to offer. This was a decade before Russians started playing in the NHL — so their best would be at the Worlds each and every year. The competition was incredible. I ended up with two bronze medals to show for my four Worlds. We won bronze in '78 and again in '83. Among the many thrills I had was scoring a goal on Vladislav Tretiak. He was the Russian equivalent of Ken Dryden, so scoring on him was a big deal for me.

Going up against the Russians was not only a thrill, it was an educational experience. I could not believe how great they were with the puck. The way they moved the puck around made me become a better passer. I realized that you're not going to score all the time, so sometimes it is better to pass it off. Once I saw how well the Russians distributed the puck, I started working really hard on that aspect of the game. Maybe it wasn't a coincidence that I finished with what was then a career high, 59 assists for the Caps, the year after my first Worlds.

I still don't think people realize just how good Europeans are at passing the puck. I know they didn't back then. Just look at Alexander Ovechkin — everyone views him as this great sniper, and he is, but he is a great passer, too.

It used to piss me off to see players whack the puck at each other. When I'm on the ice teaching at a hockey school, I love to demonstrate what I call the art of passing. It is such an important part of the game. When I'm skating toward the net on the off wing, I don't want the puck passed right in front of me. I want the puck a little bit behind me, so I can one-time it or make a move and pass it back to you. And it shouldn't be whacked at me — slide it over. There's an art to passing; I picked that up from the Europeans, and then, years later, from Gretzky, who was probably the best at it.

I scored 16 goals for Team Canada during my time at the Worlds. I even led the team with eight points in 1981. I got the chance to be teammates with Marcel Dionne, Guy Lafleur, Lanny McDonald, and Larry Robinson. Like I said, it was my Stanley Cup Final. We never won gold, but those two bronze medals still hold a special place in my heart. And yeah, I still have them.

The Worlds were about far more than just hockey. It was

I was proud to wear the red and white of Team Canada. The Worlds were my playoffs.

a chance for me to visit different countries. And with new places came new adventures. Now, remember, when I was at the Worlds, Eastern Europe was still a far-off place. The Cold War was raging. In a sense, a lot of us young Canadians on the team were travelling into the unknown.

During one tournament, our Team Canada convoy was making its way into Czechoslovakia. We had a few buses, one for management and one for partying and another one in the convoy as well. I, along with most of my teammates, was on the party bus. When we got to the border, it was all business. Armed guards came onto our bus and ordered a hammered group of young players to get out.

We did as we were told and lined up one by one along the side of our bus. Armed border police were standing a few feet away. Communist guards had guns aimed at our faces and could open fire on the lot of us at any second. We were scared as hell. Well, most of us were. One of my teammates was feeling fine — way too fine. He had passed out on the bus, and the guards could not wake him up. The guards poked him with their guns to try to wake him up, but it didn't work. Being the good teammates we were, we would not leave a man behind. We brought him out and held him up beside us in the line. We held up our passports. My inebriated friend didn't move a muscle. We held up our passed-out buddy's passport for him and showed it to the guards. I guess he looked good enough, though; we made it in to Czechoslovakia. It was one of the scariest moments of my life, and one of my teammates slept through the whole thing.

*Now, let's talk about the asterisks that you saw a couple pages back. I made my debut for Canada at the 1978 World Championship, but they were not my first Worlds. Let me explain. In 1977, for the first time ever, Canada started sending NHLers who were not going to the playoffs or who were eliminated early in the post-season to represent our country at the Worlds. In the spring of 1977, with my Barons nowhere near a playoff spot, I was asked to play for Team Canada in Vienna, Austria. I jumped at the chance, so I hopped on a plane and headed overseas.

We started playing pre-tournament games, and things were going smoothly until, an ocean away, the first round of the playoffs came to an end. Suddenly, my spot on the team was at risk. The powers that be gathered us in a room and told us, "We're bringing over a bunch of new guys and there are 10 of you who will not play in the tournament games." This would not happen nowadays; once guys commit, they get to play. But in 1977, that was not the case.

We were shocked and kind of pissed. We had come on our own time. Our wives and some of the guys' girlfriends were there.

Then Alan Eagleson came in to talk with the unlucky 10. He had a plan to calm his unimpressed troops. "Listen," the Eagle said, "we're going to send you away for a few days to have a little fun. Then we'll bring you back, put you in the team hotel. You can stay or go home, whatever you want. But if you stay, you'll have your own wine cellar, whatever wines you want. You can party. This is all on us." I decided to stay.

A few days later, the pre-tournament banquet rolled around. It was about as lavish an affair as you could get in 1977. Every team attended the banquet, and Team Canada wanted us there. And by us, I mean our newly formed posse of 10 non-playing Team Canada members. At first, we decided we were not a part of the team, so why in hell would we go to a banquet? But then we changed our tune — we 10 cast-offs all bought white pants and red-and-white shirts. We then arranged to print "Baa Baa Black Sheep" on the front of our shirts. If we were the black sheep of Team Canada, we were going to let the world, or at least everyone at the banquet, know it.

The Black Sheep decided to hit the hotel bar and let everyone at the banquet wait it out. They didn't want to start the banquet until everyone arrived, and the Black Sheep were on their own clock. We tipped back a few while the hockey world waited. Eventually someone from Team Canada got in touch with us:

The Black Sheep have arrived. Making a statement after we were banished to the press box at the Worlds. Baa Baa Baa.

"We're waiting for you guys." We finished our drinks and headed to the banquet.

By the time the Black Sheep arrived, the banquet hall was packed. The funniest part about the entire ordeal was that Team Canada was seated across the room from where we entered the hall. So in order for us to get to our table, we had to take a long walk across the hall, bypassing table after table in our "Baa Baa Black Sheep" attire. We decided to make our entrance as dramatic, and as long, as possible. One by one, we snaked through the tables to our eventual dinner spot. It took a while, but we eventually got to our seats. Score one for the Black Sheep.

All that Team Canada management did was laugh. What else could they do? They invited us to the Worlds only to tell us we couldn't play. They could have at least told us they were going to bring in more players after the first round of the playoffs before we decided to head to the tournament. But they didn't.

I was in Vienna for a month, and I didn't play one game that year. I just partied, went to games, and watched Team Canada finish fourth.

22 A NEW DAD

"As soon as he came on the ice for a shift, people would start with the chant, "Maaruuuk." It sounded like they were booing him, but they were just calling his name."

— Joni

When it was time to lace up for my second season with the Caps, I wasn't just playing for Joni, my teammates, and myself: I was playing for little Jon Dennis Maruk as well. Our first child was born on July 14, 1979, in Prince George's, Maryland. Jon was an incredible gift for Joni and me. We had a beautiful, healthy baby boy. I'll admit, Jon wasn't all that pretty at the start; he came out with a football head. He kind of looked like E.T., but the football head lasted only for a couple of days.

Life was a lot different back in 1979. Joni and Jon had to stay in the hospital for a couple of days after the birth. At one point, Rick Green called. My Caps teammate was single at the time. He asked me what I was up to, and I told him I was at the hospital with my wife and new baby boy. "Do you want to come see the kid?" I asked. "No, no, no," Rick said. And then, without missing a beat, he added, "Meet me downtown. Let's go have a beer."

I told Joni that Rick wanted to go for a few. "Go ahead," she said. We did that a few times.

Being a dad changed me. Jon gave me a much better outlook on life. And he made me a better hockey player as well. You would think that being a dad would soften me up on the ice, but that was not the case. I realized that my job as a player was very important. I had to look after my wife and kid. I had to take care of this little guy. There was more to my life and my career — I was suddenly a provider. And if I was going to be the best provider possible, I had to be the best player possible.

But my second season with the Caps did not go as planned. It was pretty much over before it started. And that's too bad because I got off to a great start in the fall of '79. We got our first win of the season in our third game of the year. We beat the Rangers 5–3. It was one of those nights where everything went right for me. I scored four goals, and through the first three games of the season I had six. I continued to find the back of the net over the next couple of weeks, and by the time we pulled into Vancouver on October 27, I had seven goals and three assists for 10 points in the first seven games of the year. Then it all went wrong.

I scored a short-handed goal early in the second to tie the game up at two. Then a few minutes later, I assisted on a goal by Tom Rowe, and we were up 3–2. Then my season was turned upside down.

I wasn't the only undersized high-scoring forward on the ice that night in Vancouver. The Canucks had a second-year player out of Sweden named Thomas Gradin. He was a couple of inches taller than me, but he tipped the scales at only 170 pounds. He was coming off a pretty impressive rookie season — he had 51 points in 76 games for the Canucks in 1977–78. On this night though, it wasn't his offensive upside that took my season off the rails. It was his knee.

Thomas Gradin and I collided at the blue line. It wasn't a check. It wasn't a dirty hit. It was just a knee-on-knee collision. The play was offside, so I stayed on the ice to take the faceoff. I wasn't feeling that great, but I didn't think it was that bad. Then I went to take the draw. As soon as I put pressure on my left knee to take the faceoff, the pain shot through me — something was very wrong.

I went into our dressing room and it was bad news. My knee was a mess. The official diagnosis was a torn MCL. While the rest of my teammates continued on to Edmonton for a game the next night, I went right back to Washington. The next day, I was on an operating table as a bunch of doctors tried to salvage my MCL.

I woke up from surgery to find a giant cast on my left leg. It started at the top of my leg and went all the way down to my ankle. My leg was bent, too, in kind of a hook, so the MCL would heal properly. I had nowhere to go. All I could do was lie around. It was a tough time, but what can you do? You're a hockey player. It's part of the business.

I've always had a high pain tolerance. If you think of an injury, chances are I've had it and tried to play through it: torn MCLs, foot tendonitis, dislocated shoulders, and who knows what else. Not too long ago, I was playing in a charity game and the mayor of the town — he was about 6-foot-4, 250 pounds — fell right on top of me. I finished the game. Two days later, I wasn't feeling all that fine. I went to the hospital to get checked out. I had two broken ribs. A buddy of mine thought I was out of my mind finishing a charity game with two broken ribs. Imagine if he ever found out that I travelled to the Maritimes later that week for five more charity games. I taped up my ribs and played through the pain. They had me advertised in the program, so I felt I had to show up.

23 GUITAR TOWN

"He loves music and he loves to dance. He's very passionate about music. We've all said that if he didn't play hockey, he should have been some sort of dancer or musician."

— Sarah Maruk, Dennis's daughter

I wasn't one for sitting around. After about three or four days, I'd had enough. I got up and headed for the door, jumped into my gigantic black Cadillac, and went shopping. I'm sure it was quite a sight, this 5-foot-8 man, driving a giant 3,000-pound Caddy with the seat jammed as far back as possible, so his ripped-apart leg in a cast could fit in the driver's seat. Anyway, my shopping trip resulted in my buying a guitar. I had to do something to kill the time, so I started picking away. It was my first foray into the world of music. I signed up for guitar lessons. I'd jump into my Caddy, cast and all, and head off to guitar class. It kept me busy. Like I said, rehab in the '70s was a little different. The guitar lessons stopped as soon as my leg healed. I never went back.

I still love music, though. If hockey is my game, then music is my passion. I was never scared on the ice, but learning to play guitar, learning to play music, scared me. Going up against a 225-pound defenceman? No problem. Going up onstage and playing an instrument? Big problem. I still have a guitar at home, but I haven't been able to take the leap and dive into it full time. It's the fear of failure.

My friend Brian Good still shows me chords from time to time. He'll just kind of chuckle when I try to crank out a tune. I really think I could've become a rock musician. I would have liked to be Angus Young in AC/DC, leaping around the stage. I see that and think, *Man, I'd love to do that.*

I know what you may be thinking: *What in the hell are you afraid of? You played hockey in front of 18,000 people. Pick up your guitar.* But it's not that easy for me. I was gifted in one area, hockey. But with the guitar? Not so much.

That's not to say I haven't been onstage before. A few years ago at a Grey Cup party, I jumped up onstage with Brian and started playing the bongos. I told Brian I wanted to play guitar, but he told me, "No, play the bongos." I'll give Brian credit — I may know hockey, but he knows music. The bongos and I connected. He had seen me play them before, and his advance scouting paid off. I ended up playing with Brian and the guys onstage for an hour and a half. I was right in there on every song. I was just like a drummer, keeping the beat, being loud when I had to be, taking it easy when that's what the song called for.

Maybe I had found my second calling. When things settled down, Brian said, "You're not a guitar player, you're a bongo player. One time we stopped, and you just kept going. We're impressed." What do you know, my first solo.

Dancing up a storm at my son Jon's wedding (and eventually winning the dance off against Jon). Music has always been a passion.

I still wouldn't mind playing the guitar, though, even if I'm destined to be a bongo player. Hey, I wanted to play for the Leafs when I was a kid, but I guess I was destined to play for the Seals, Barons, and Capitals. You just have to make the most with what you have.

24 CHASING 50

"He had the old tuck and drag, way ahead of his time.
He'd pull the puck into his feet and then go upstairs on the
goalie."

— Greg Theberge, Washington Capitals defenceman

I came back from my MCL injury toward the end of the 1979–80 season, and I finished with 27 points in 27 games. Once again, the Capitals did not make the playoffs, but I didn't play in the Worlds in the spring of 1980 — my knee was still healing.

I was fully recovered by the time the next season rolled around. We had some good young players on our Caps team, like Mike Gartner and Ryan Walter, but our head coach Gary Green decided to put me on a line with a couple of veteran wingers. I was the guy in the middle for 29-year-old Bob "Hound" Kelly and 34-year-old Jean Pronovost. The Hound Dog joined the Caps that year after a decade in Philly, where he won two Cups with the Broad Street Bullies. The 1980–81 season would be Jean's final full NHL campaign. He finished his career with 774 points in 998 regular-season games.

Soon enough, Kelly, Pronovost, and I were dubbed "the Roaring 20s Line." We all wore numbers in the 20s, so why not. And early in the 1980–81 season we were roaring indeed. On November 15, 1980, I scored three goals in an 8–4 Caps win in Hartford. The Roaring 20s combined for eight points. It was my second hat trick in as many games, and I was the first Cap to ever do that. I also extended my point streak to 10 games, tying a Caps record. (The streak ended at 10, though, coming to a close in our next game a few nights later versus Quebec). The entire team was playing better, too.

If you picked up a newspaper on December 1, 1980, the Washington Capitals were at 8-6-9 in the season, ninth in the NHL standings! I was seventh in the league scoring race as November came to a close. Unfortunately for us, those numbers weren't sustainable. We cooled down considerably.

How much did we cool off? Well, in the January 24, 1981, edition of the *Washington Post*, under the headline "Roaring 20s in Depression," Robert Fachet started his column this way:

> *Q. In the last 10 games each has played, who has scored the most points — Mike Palmateer, Dennis Maruk, Jean Pronovost, or Bob Kelly?*
>
> *A. Palmateer, three.*

That's right, we were being outscored by a goalie. The team was clinging onto fourth place in the Patrick Division. With three games to go in the regular season, we were in the fight

With the late Tom Lysiak at the 1978 World Hockey Championships. RIP Tom.
He was a great hockey player who is greatly missed.

of our lives for the final playoff spot — 16th overall — in the
NHL. I scored my 46th of the season against the Boston Bruins
and assisted on the Hound's game winner on April 2. We were
tied with the Leafs for the 16th and final spot with two games
to go. We dropped our next game to the eventual Stanley Cup
champions, the New York Islanders, 4–1. We needed a win over
Detroit in our final game of the regular season and a Nordiques
win over the Leafs. If both of those things happened, I'd finally
get my first taste of NHL playoff hockey.

25 THE SAME OLD SITUATION

"Dennis always seemed to be able to get the puck at the right time. He had a quick release and a good shot. He had a real knack for being at the right place . . . and most of those places were around the net."

— Mike Gartner, Hockey Hall of Famer, 708 career goals

I wish I could tell you what I did against the Detroit Red Wings on April 5, 1981, but I have no recollection of the night. That's kind of strange when you look at the game summary and see what happened. Glen Currie gave us a 1–0 lead just 11 seconds into the first period. It seems we were a determined bunch. I also scored two in the first, and we went into the dressing room with a 4–1 lead. A Caps win looked inevitable. Only two questions remained: Would the Nordiques beat the Leafs? Would I get 50? Well, one of the two happened that night, just not the one that sent us to the playoffs.

Just over 13 minutes into the third period, I scored my 50th and final goal of the 1980–81 season. The game summary shows I beat Wings 'tender Larry Lozinski. It was the final game of his 30-game NHL career. I have absolutely no memory of my 50th goal whatsoever. Not so much as a sniff. If video exists, I haven't seen it. I have heard an audio call by Caps play-by-play announcer Ron Weber. "The puck now is Kelly's. Right rear boards, skates out front, passes it in front, and Maruk has scored! Dennis Maruk — another hat trick! And Washington has it 6–2. Dennis Maruk's 50th goal of the year." The old horn is blaring in the background. When the PA announcer made the announcement, the crowd did its usual thing and rained down "Maruuuuuuuuk" from the rafters. Fifty: history shows it happened.

Maybe it's burned into the memory of one of the 12,531 who were in attendance. Maybe my teammates who picked up the assists on the goal, the Hound or Howard Walker, recall it. But I don't. We eventually won the game 7–2. Maybe I don't recall the goal because there was nothing to celebrate that night.

Over in Toronto, the team I grew up cheering for as a kid, the Leafs, beat the Nordiques 4–2. We didn't know the outcome of the Toronto game until our game was finished. Our head coach Gary Green wouldn't allow the public address announcer in our building to give updates on what was going on in Toronto. He didn't want us to be distracted from the task at hand. Once our game was over, we found out what was happening in Toronto. We missed the playoffs by one point. It was crushing. As I told Robert Fachet in his post-game wrap-up for the *Washington Post*, "Fifty means nothing to me now. The playoffs were everything." I had just finished my sixth NHL season, and I was still waiting to play in my first NHL playoff game.

Looking back, I'm very proud to have scored 50 goals that year and honoured to join an exclusive club. But it must be old age setting in because I have no recollection of the milestone. All I remember is that from February 1 until the end of the season we went 8-15-6. Maybe the year ending the way it did, just a single point from making the playoffs, helped to erase the memory of my first 50-goal season.

26 FINDING MY GROOVE

"Because of his size, the pressure was on him to make an
impact at every level — to score goals, to rack up points.
So that was his focus. A lot of people maybe saw that as a
detriment. I saw it as a huge asset. Our goal was to get him
the puck as much as possible. Every once in a while, Dennis
and I would switch off in the defensive zone. I'd try to play
a little bit of defence for him, so he could take the puck and
go."

— Ryan Walter, Dennis's linemate in 1981–82

When people meet me, they want to talk about my 60-goal season. I scored 60 in 1981–82, but the season got off to anything but a magical start. We split our first two games of the year and then things went bad — really bad. Now, remember, we had just missed the playoffs by a single point, so we had expectations. What we didn't expect was that we'd lose 13 games in a row between mid-October and mid-November, but that's what happened. Fifteen games into the season, we were 1-14. The start cost our coach Gary Green his job; he was let go after a 6–1 loss to Minnesota. Roger Crozier stepped behind the bench and then Bryan Murray came in. Bryan stuck around for a long time.

Bryan was my last coach with the Caps, and he was the best I ever played for. In the simplest terms, Bryan Murray understood his players. He knew who you would click with on the ice and he respected your talent. When Bryan came into the fold, we slowly started to turn our season around. With him behind the bench, we finally snapped out of our losing streak. I scored my 10th of the season in a 3–3 tie against the Wings. The next night, we finally got a win. I scored a shorty and added an assist, and Dave Parro made a whopping 44 saves as we beat the Whalers 4–0. It was our first of four wins in a row. During that streak, we destroyed the Rockies 7–1 and the Flyers 10–4. We scored 17 goals in two games. Tim Tookey and I each had a hat trick in that win over the Flyers. Suddenly the Caps were on a roll.

We kept on winning. I scored four goals and tied a team record with six points in a 7–3 win over the Jets on December 4. I was scoring and the Caps were winning — what was going on? It all started against the Wings on November 13. That innocent little tie began a streak that saw us go 8-3-2 over the next month. We had dug ourselves a hole with our start, but we were playing solid hockey and climbing back into the playoff picture. Unfortunately, that didn't last. We went 1-7-1 for the rest of December.

While the team was floundering, the puck kept going in the net for me. By the time the calendar changed to 1982, I had 27 goals. Not that anyone noticed outside of D.C., though — that Gretzky kid I had met in my parents' backyard after my rookie season had 50. He set an all-time record on December 30 by scoring his 50th in just 39 games.

I was humming along with new linemates that season. Murray put me with Ryan Walter on one side and Chris Valentine on the other. Chris had started the year in Hershey, but when they called him up and put him with me and Ryan, we all clicked. Chris was only 19; Ryan was 23 — I was the old man on the line at 25. We gelled right away and Bryan Murray kept us together.

We were three very different players who complemented each other very well. We got a lot of ice time, in all kinds of situations. Ryan, our young captain, was a hard-hitting left-winger. He'd go in the corners and just bang away, creating a lot of loose pucks in the process. Then I or Chris would go in and fish it out. Together, we'd create a lot of scoring opportunities because we were both very good passers and could score. Ryan could put the puck in the net as well, but he was viewed around the league as more of an aggressive, tough-hitting guy. He opened up a lot of space.

The three of us wanted to win so badly. It's just that our team was missing a couple of key components. We kept racking up the goals. I guess we thought that if we could lead the team offensively, maybe management would make a few trades and bring some guys in to fill the holes we had. Strangely enough, they didn't make that trade until just before the next season, and it involved Ryan Walter. He and Rick Green went to the Canadiens for Rod Langway, Brian Engblom, Doug Jarvis, and Craig Laughlin. The Caps had to get rid of something to get something. It hurt losing a linemate, but it was a great move for the team. The move changed our defensive core, which was really struggling, and that made a big difference. But at the beginning of 1982, that Ryan Walter trade was still nine months away. We had to find a way to keep scoring, and the Caps had to find a way to start winning — fast — or there would be no playoffs for us ... again.

27 MR. PRESIDENT

"What sticks in my mind even more than Dennis going to the White House is the fact that they gave him a microphone on the day of the All-Star Game. I remember we were laughing about him being taped that day . . . Just watch your language.""

— Joni

I was the new kid on the block. We were in Buffalo, New York, at the 1978 All-Star Game. It was my first appearance. I was representing the Cleveland Barons and suiting up for the Wales Conference. In the dressing room, I was sitting with the best in the game. My All-Star teammates included Guy Lafleur, Larry Robinson, Darryl Sittler, Marcel Dionne, Lanny McDonald, and Gilbert Perreault, and our head coach, Scotty Bowman. I remember thinking, *And here's Dennis Maruk from Rexdale, Ontario — what are you doing here?* I didn't feel very comfortable sitting with all those great players. But that's also when I realized, *You made it.* I had achieved something. I was good enough to skate with the best.

We didn't have a lot of time to socialize at the All-Star Game in the '70s. It's not like today, where there's a skills competition and a lot of hanging around, and they have three days to chat and socialize. We had about a day and a half. We'd fly in, attend a banquet, have a few drinks, maybe a little party, and then get up the next day and play the game. Most guys also had their families with them, so there wasn't a lot of time for any deep, get-to-know-you conversations.

The other thing about the 1978 All-Star Game: it was a *real game*. I know that may be tough to comprehend now, but there used to be hitting and digging and backchecking. Perreault scored the OT winner, and we beat the Campbell Conference 3–2.

Four years later, I'd play in my second and final All-Star Game. I was a hell of a lot more comfortable the second time there. The NHL held the 1982 All-Star Game in Washington, D.C. Only one Capital was named to the Wales Conference team, and I was the lucky representative. Unlike in 1978, I wasn't at all intimidated. Al Arbour, coach of the New York Islanders, named me to the Wales squad on February 2; the game was in Washington on February 9. He also named his own player John Tonelli to the team. He chose Tonelli over Ryan Walter. That made for a pretty big story in Washington.

For me, it was much more than a game this time around. We were at the Capital Centre, and I was the only Cap on the team. I was going to get my fair share of press. In fact, I had a camera crew follow me around for a good chunk of that week. They got all kinds of footage, including a ton of tape of me and my dad, John, and mother, Anne, driving to the rink to share the ice with the likes of Gretzky and Bossy. (By the time the All-Star Game rolled around, Gretzky was leading the league with 69 goals, 83 assists, and 152 points. *At the All-Star break.* More than 60 points behind, I was fourth in league scoring with 41 goals and 50 assists.)

Having my mom and dad there was such a big thrill. As I told the *Washington Post* before the game,

> *"Being named to an All-Star team is always a thrill, but this is something special. My mother and father are here — they didn't make it last time. And I'm sure, playing in front of the home crowd, I'll be pumped up."*

However, before the game, there was still some business I had to take care of. Now, if I thought I didn't belong in the same room with guys like Lafleur and Dionne in 1978, how do you think I would feel dining at the White House? On February 8, the day before the All-Star Game, a group of mostly young Canadian kids who made up both the Wales and Campbell Conference All-Star teams joined Ronald Reagan, the president of the United States, for lunch.

We strolled into the White House in our best attire. The security was very tight. Reagan got up at one point and made a speech. He said, "I just wanted to let the Edmonton Oilers know that we just made a trade." He paused for a little bit for dramatic effect. "We just made a trade with Edmonton for Wayne Gretzky. The problem is we have to give up the state of Texas."

Everybody had a good laugh. I'm not sure if a lot of guys with a Fu Manchu had lunch at the White House, but my 'stache was looking its best that day. After lunch, we all got in line to meet the president. All I remember is shaking hands with Reagan and saying, "I'm Dennis from the Washington Capitals." I don't really remember what Reagan said back, but it was a pretty cool experience. Again, there I was in yet another place I wasn't supposed to be. Little Dennis from Rexdale, too small to play junior, too small to play in the NHL, breaking bread with the president of the United States. It's amazing where the game can take you.

28 SHIVERS

*"I was sitting with his parents . . . he was a fan favourite,
there was no doubt. He'd really made it. I was filled with
pride, as were his mom and dad."*

— Joni

The next night, it was time to put away the suit and strap on the blades. Just to show you how much things have changed over the years, here are a few facts about that night in Landover: Tickets ranged from 10 bucks all the way up to a whopping $17.50. Note the decimal point — that's $17.50, not $1,750.00. And the night before the game you could still get tickets. And if you wanted to watch the morning skate, you just drove out to Maryland — it was free to get in to watch the NHL All-Stars practise.

One of the coolest things about playing in an All-Star Game is the player introductions. It is a chance for the fans to salute you and for you to salute the fans. Before the game, I was pretty sure the Caps fans were going to be overly nice to me, but I did not expect what I got.

We lined up for the intros. I was going to be the last player introduced on the Wales Conference team. All these great players from both teams were lined up before me, and I mean all-time superstars: Gretzky, Trottier, and Bossy, Dale Hawerchuk, Randy Carlyle, and Peter Stastny. I waited, wondering, *What will going last be like?* I was so nervous.

We went out on the ice and lined up at our blue lines. Now, I've mentioned a number of times having no recollection of big moments in my life. Well, the 1982 All-Star Game player introductions is one of the few moments from my career that is easy to find on YouTube. It's right there for everyone to see. The guys from the Campbell Conference line up on the ice first and then it's our turn. Before I even go onto the ice, you can hear the chants of "Maruuuuuuuk" from the crowd. Then we take our spots on the blue line. For the next six minutes, the players are introduced. Things begin with the Campbell Conference starters. Wayne Gretzky gets a nice ovation from the crowd when he is introduced.

Then it's our turn. The first member of the Wales Conference to be introduced is our goaltender Michel Dion. Down the line they go, slowly building up to the last guy in line — me. Standing right beside me is Marc Tardif from the Quebec Nordiques, and after he is introduced, you can hear it again. "Maruuuuuuuuuk." The camera pans to me and I have an almost-embarrassed look on my face. I'm clearly happy, but a little overwhelmed by the attention. By the time the PA announcer belts out, "From the Washington Capitals . . ." the crowd is already on its feet.

To have those Caps fans stand up and applaud me at the All-Star Game was such an honour. They were so supportive of me, for my accomplishments and what I had done as a member of the Capitals. The applause rained down, and it was an absolutely incredible feeling. The camera switched back to me, and you can just tell how proud I am. It was a fantastic moment. And what made it even better was that my parents were there to share it. It was a big moment for them, too. "I knew there would be cheers," I told the *Washington Post* after the game, "but I didn't expect the chants to last so long."

I tried to settle down, but my nerves were jumping. Eventually, I did relax, and the Caps fans and my mom and dad got to see me record my first All-Star point. I picked up an assist when I set up Ray Bourque to tie it 1–1 in the first. According to that same *Washington Post* article, my old buddy Gilles Meloche robbed me on a golden chance to score as well. We won my second and final All-Star Game 4–2.

29 THE ROAD TO 60

"It was exciting . . . by and large the best performance by a Cap, period. We were thrilled by the pursuit of 60."

— Steve Mehlman, longtime Caps season-ticket holder

Once I woke up from my All-Star Weekend dream, it was back to business for me and the Caps. We started the final half of the season with a six-game western road trip. On the first game of the swing, I picked up right where I left off with two goals and an assist in a 5–3 win over the Flames. I had seven goals in my previous three games.

But the roll I was on was nothing compared with what Wayne Gretzky was doing that season. My exploits were big news in Washington, but the hockey world had its eyes on Gretzky. After he scored his 50th in 39 games before the new year, everyone was wondering how many goals he would score in total. It seemed like only a matter of time before he would break Phil Esposito's single-season record of 77. The question was how many would he get beyond that?

I got to see Gretzky in action one night after our win in Calgary. We flew into Edmonton to take on the Oilers. I scored my 44th of the season in a 5–3 loss. Gretzky scored his 70th and added two assists to push his season points total to 155. Mr. Gretzky was in a league of his own.

In our fifth game of the road trip, I scored numbers 48 and 49. The 48th gave me 100 points on the year. But again, if you were to ask me to recall the magical moment, I couldn't. The only description I could find is from Robert Fachet's post-game write-up in the February 21, 1982, edition of the *Washington Post*:

> *"It took Maruk, a Minnesota cast off, only 28 seconds to reach the century mark. Randy Holt sent the puck in from the left point and Gartner deflected it to Maruk in the right-wing circle. He easily beat Gilles Meloche while defenceman Gordie Roberts stared without moving a few feet away."*

It must have been a quick release. That night, I became the first Capital to get 100 points in a season. But as Fachet also pointed out, there was not much reason to celebrate. We lost 7–3 and were 11 points back from Pittsburgh for the fourth spot in the Patrick Division.

Earning 100 points or scoring 50 goals in the best league in the world was an honour. It was big. But even bigger would have been making the playoffs. You need to have personal pride and a fear of failure to be a successful athlete. Not making the playoffs was a failure. I always thought I was helping our team by scoring goals; the more I scored, the better chance we had of winning. Sure, other teams might have said, "We have to watch this guy," but when you score 50 goals and your season is over after 80 games, it can all feel pretty meaningless when your ultimate goal is to win the Stanley Cup.

I wish I had more to say about the milestone moments — I really do. But it's all a blur. The next day in Winnipeg, I hit the 50-goal mark for the second year in a row. I added a 51st as well. We won 6–3 that day in the 'Peg and finished our six-game road trip with a 3-3 record. Going back to before the All-Star Game, I had scored in eight straight and tied a club record set by Mike Gartner. I scored 15 goals in those eight games. The streak came to an end in, get this, a 9–1 win over the Blues in our first game back from our road trip.

I had 51 for the season and the pursuit of 60 was on. Before February 1982, only six men in hockey history had amassed 60 in a campaign. Phil Esposito, Guy Lafleur, Reggie Leach, Steve Shutt, Mike Bossy, and Wayne Gretzky were all part of an exclusive club. Gretzky was the newest member — he had scored his 60th earlier in the season — and, soon enough, I would join them.

30 60

"Sixty goals is a pretty unique thing. There are only so many guys who have done it. I think because of where Dennis played, there wasn't a lot of attention paid in Washington then, not like there is now. So I think that maybe people don't think of Dennis Maruk right away when they think of 50- and 60-goal scorers."

— Mike Gartner

By the time we pulled into Toronto for our second-last game of the season, our playoff hopes were long gone. And that meant that once again, I would not be going to the post-season. It was the same old same old, but at least on this night there was a bit of a storyline to follow.

For a while, the hockey world was wondering if Wayne Gretzky would score 100 goals in 1981–82. He didn't hit the century mark, but he finished with an incredible 92 goals and 212 points. Both shattered the old NHL records. With numbers like that, and Mike Bossy hitting the 60-goal mark earlier that season, you can see why I was flying under the radar in my pursuit of 60. When we got to Toronto on April 3, I had 58 goals and two games left to join the 60 club.

As I've said before, playing in Toronto was always very special for me. It meant a chance to visit my family at our place in Rexdale and then hopefully impress them at Maple Leaf Gardens. Plus, as a bonus this time around, it was a Saturday night, which meant the Washington Capitals were making a rare appearance on *Hockey Night in Canada*. What a great night this would be to score number 60.

History shows I scored number 59 against Doug Favell on a power play with just over three minutes to go in the first to tie the game at one. I scored number 60 with 2:01 to go in the second. My linemates, Ryan Walter and Chris Valentine, picked up the assists. Now if you're looking for a play-by-play recount of the big goal — I don't have it for you. I never sit around telling people about number 60 because, as per usual, I can't remember it. I wish I did. I don't remember the goals. What I do remember is that I had a chance to score more that night and in the final game of the season against Montreal. I remember the chances. I swear I could have scored 75 or 80 goals that year — I had so many chances, missed so many other opportunities, night after night.

I was a 60-goal man, but it's not like the hockey world blew open my doors wanting to find out more about my magical season. The *Globe and Mail* had a headline the next day that read "Maruk gains 60-goal plateau." The only quote from me in the story was about us missing the playoffs.

The *Washington Post* ran a story in the bottom right-hand

corner of the front page of their sports section: "Maruk scores 60th as Capitals win, 6–4." The fact that I scored 60 wasn't all that remarkable, simply because it seemed to be the stylish thing to do that season. This is what Bill Walker wrote in the *Post*:

> *With 60 goals, Maruk joins Wayne Gretzky of the Edmonton Oilers and Mike Bossy of the New York Islanders as the only NHL players to reach 60 goals this season.*

In the story, it seemed I was more bummed about missing the playoffs than I was pumped about reaching 60.

> *"I'd give a few of those goals back to make the playoffs one of these years. I'd like to see what it's like."*

So my 60 goals didn't get a lot of play outside of D.C. It makes sense when you think about it — Gretzky was in a whole other world. Mike Bossy, Peter Stastny, and I were in a race to see who would wind up second in the goal-scoring race, but what Gretzky was doing was unbelievable. He deserved to get the attention.

I can't recall if the lack of attention bothered me at the time, but this is what I will say to you today. Yes, my 60 goals were put on the back burner. People have come up to me over the years and have said, "Look at the season you had: 60 goals, 76 assists, 136 points!" But then I tell them to look at what Gretzky was doing. The Oilers had such a terrific team; they had so much talent. He scored 92 goals and more than 200 points. *That* is an unbelievable year.

No one has ever scored 60 for the Leafs. The only two guys to score 60 for Montreal are Lafleur and Shutt. Perhaps if I had scored my 60 wearing a Maple Leafs uniform or a Habs jersey, it would have been a bigger deal.

31 GO OVIE

*"[To have Dad mentioned with Ovechkin] is pretty unique.
It's pretty cool. He's obviously in an elite class. There are
not many players who have put up the numbers that Dad
did. He's still got the record for assists and points for the
Capitals."*

— Jon Maruk, Dennis's son

These days, I don't go around telling people I'm a 60-goal scorer.
It is by no means how I introduce myself. If people bring it up,
I'll talk about it, but to be honest I didn't really give my 60 goals
all that much thought until just a few years ago. I was in a celeb-
rity golf tournament and one of the guys in my group was really
excited to play with me. He pulled out a sheet of the leading
scorers from the 1981–82 season. In order, the top seven scorers
that year were Gretzky, Bossy, Stastny, Maruk, Trottier, Savard,
Dionne; three Hall of Famers in front of me and three Hall of
Famers right behind me. Dennis Maruk from Rexdale, fourth
in the NHL scoring race in 1981–82 with 136 points. My golf

partner pointed to my name and said, "You're in pretty good company there. That's amazing." I guess that's when it kind of hit me — I did something pretty special that season.

When I got out of hockey, I began a different life. I was a deckhand on a boat, a bellhop in a high-end Aspen hotel, and a farmhand for a rock star. For years, 60 was a far-off distant memory, if even that.

As I got older, though, I started thinking about what I did on the ice more and more. That's probably because people started asking me about it more often. When I moved back to Toronto, I'd get introduced to people as "Dennis. He scored 60 goals one year." It just pops up more in conversation now than it did when I initially left hockey.

When Alexander Ovechkin broke my Caps record with 65 goals in 2007–08, I was still off the hockey radar. I was skiing in Aspen, and I'd get calls from reporters asking me what I was up to. The Caps didn't fly me in to see Ovie break my record, but I kept a close eye on things. I was having a beer and lunch at the bottom of a hill in Aspen when I got the call that Ovechkin broke my record. I told the reporter that I was very happy for Ovie — I had been cheering him on. I was disappointed that the Caps didn't have me around to witness Ovechkin score his 60th and 61st goals. I would have loved to have been there to pass the torch to Alex. To me, he's the most exciting and electrifying player in the game.

Ovie broke my goals record with the Caps, but I'm not sure if anyone is ever going to break my points record of 136. But if they do, I'd love to be there to see it. I guess if I lived around D.C., the Caps would invite me. But they didn't seem all that

With Alexander Ovechkin, who broke my Caps Record when he scored 65 goals for Washington in the 2007–08 season. It was an honour to have a player like Ovie break my team goal-scoring record.

keen on flying me in and paying for a hotel to see Alex break my goals record. Anyway, very few guys in today's game are going to break 136 points. The Caps and I are back on better footing as of late, though. They flew me down recently to honour me as one of their top 40 players of all time. That was nice. I got to meet a few season-ticket holders; a few of them were even around back in my day. They played a video of some of my highlights on the

Jumbotron. I was all decked out in my suit and hat. I gave a wave to the crowd. They gave me a standing ovation. It was pretty special. I'd like to do more with the Caps, but what can you do.

As of this writing, I'm on a pretty exclusive list. Only 20 players have scored 60 goals in an NHL season. I was the seventh player to do it. The names on that list are huge: Gretzky, Lemieux, Brett Hull, Bobby Hull, Esposito, Lafleur, and then, at an even 60, there's me. A lot of people see my name and go, "Who is that guy?" It's kind of funny. I'll be at an event and I will say to my table, "All right, we're going to write down a list of players who scored 60 goals in an NHL season." They come up with the usual suspects — 13 or 14 names — and then they're stumped as to who the final few are. I'll give them a couple of hints. Finally, they'll look at me and say, "You?" Yep, me. It's funny, people usually name off everyone except me and Bernie Nicholls. We are usually the last two.

I don't lose much sleep over the fact that I'm often overlooked on that list of 60-goal scorers; I'm just happy I'm on it. The fact that people recall it is an honour. It is something I didn't think about for a long time — remember, I went off the hockey radar for a while. I was working on a boat in the middle of the Gulf of Mexico — you don't chat about hockey much out there. The 60 goals were part of my hockey life, and that season is very memorable. But so is my life off the ice. You remember Hall and Oates, don't you? Great band. Well, for a while it was Maruk and Oates.

My first rep team. I made the jump from house league after my first year of organized hockey. Future pro Gary Carr is our goalie. I'm sitting far left in the first row.

Me as a Knights rookie on the shoulders of future NHLer Dennis Ververgaert, our
goalie Peter Crosbie, and captain Reggie Thomas, who played in the NHL and
WHA. I was the 1972–73 OHA Rookie of the Year. I had 113 points in 59 games.

I was reluctant to go to London but was all smiles at the end of the year. Here I am with a couple of pieces of hardware, the OHA and London Knights top rookie awards, after year number one.

1975 — My first year in the NHL, playing for the California Golden Seals.

A great-looking group at the 1979 World Championships. I'm surrounded by a fun and talented bunch. Left to right in the front row, that's Trevor Johansen, Brad Maxwell, me, and a smiling, tongue waggling Wilf Paiement. Back row left to right is Al MacAdam, David Shand, Robert Picard, and Dale McCourt.

The 3M Line in action against the Buffalo Sabres. Left to right, that's Al MacAdam, me at centre, and Bobby Murdoch. As a trio, we combined for 174 points in 1975–76.

Fighting for the puck against future Hall of Famer Marcel Dionne. Playing against Marcel pushed me to be a better hockey player. He, like me, was overlooked throughout his hockey career.

At the Forum against Guy Lafleur. It was an honour to play against one of the greatest Habs and NHL players of all time.

Notice the short stick? It made for better puck control. It wasn't the longest twig, but it did some damage. Credit: Bob Shaver/Hockey Hall of Fame

When I lined up with Team Canada, I was honoured to call guys like Guy Lafleur, Lanny McDonald, and Larry Robinson my teammates. I scored 16 goals for Canada at four tournaments.

Team Canada 1981. Our head coach, the great Don Cherry, is in the middle. I'm right in front of him.

My signature look — a scowl, the Fu Manchu, and my scoring weapon in hand.

32 MARUK AND OATES

"He mentioned to me once that he was helping out with John Oates."

— Jon Maruk, Dennis's son

For about 20 years after I scored 60, I was a hard man to find. I was still surrounded by snow and ice, but I was in Aspen, Colorado, a long way from the NHL. If you were looking for some high-end furniture and service with a smile from a former 60-goal scorer, I was your man. I got the job thanks to hockey. I was coaching a high school team, and the dad of one of the players owned the furniture store. He was looking for someone to run his warehouse, and I got the job.

Dennis Maruk, just the seventh man in NHL history to score 60 goals in an NHL season, was in the mountains of Colorado, selling furniture to the stars. A famous Hollywood actress was a client — a really nice lady. She bought a massive chandelier from our store one day; the thing had to cost somewhere between 30 and 40 thousand dollars.

When she came in to look around, the first thing she wanted to know was "Anywhere I can go for a smoke?" At that time, I had developed a pretty decent habit and was putting down anywhere from half a pack to a pack a day. I looked at the woman and said, "Sure, come with me." I led the lady out back and we had a smoke. My puffing partner was Goldie Hawn. We got to talking and we had a lot to chat about. Her son was a goaltender, so we talked a little hockey. They had a nice place about 15 minutes outside of Aspen.

I delivered the chandelier to their house and helped to set it up. I pulled up to Goldie and Kurt Russell's place; they had a lovely log cabin with all kinds of horses. It was beautiful and all decked out for the Christmas season.

I went into the house and Goldie said, "Come on upstairs." I took a second to think about things, then blurted out, just for clarification, "You want me to go upstairs?" Get your mind out of the gutter, Dennis!

"Kate's coming for Christmas, and we gotta fix up her room." Okay, things were starting to make a lot more sense to me now. Goldie needed me to help fix up her daughter Kate Hudson's room.

So we go up and I start making notes. She says, "I need a new bed. I have to get a table for a laptop. This isn't right, you know."

Of course, I asked, "When's Kate coming?" Hey, I was a single guy . . .

Goldie bought a bunch of stuff for Kate's room. We delivered all of it out to their place, and I made sure I didn't miss that delivery. I never did get to meet Kate, but her mom was wonderful. She even signed a magazine cover for me. I framed it and still have it.

Goldie was one of the first high-profile clients I met at our store, but she was not the last. One day, John Oates, from Hall and Oates, came into the store. He needed some help out on his farm just outside of Aspen and asked the storeowner, Paul, if there was anyone available. Paul told John that he had a guy named Dennis who had weekends off, so he sent me out to the farm.

That weekend, I pulled up to a beautiful farm on the outskirts of Aspen. There was a fantastic apple orchard and all kinds of animals: llamas, peacocks, everything. John was right there to greet me. "How ya doing? I hear you're a hockey player," he said. I shot back, "I hear you're a musician." We hit it off right away.

John Oates and I got to work on his farm. He said, "I've got some machinery to move and I've got my tractor. I want you to guide and we'll hook up to the tractor." I said, "No problem." I must have done a pretty decent job because he had more work for me. "You wouldn't mind coming and helping me move some stuff over here?"

Then he looked at me and said, "How much time do you have?" I said, "All day and all weekend." We did a few chores around his farm, and then he asked me how much cash I wanted for helping him out. "I don't know," I told John. "You pay me what you think I'm worth." He said, "How about 75 bucks an hour?" Maybe I should have been negotiating my own contracts during my playing years. It was a decent payday.

John asked me to come out to his farm the next day to give him a hand again. Then he asked me to come back and help clear some dead trees from his orchard on Wednesday. Then he asked me if I knew anything about landscaping. Like the goals did back in 1982, the offers were coming in bunches from John Oates. "Do you mind coming out for a couple of hours after work and helping me?" Not at all, I said. I was happy to help; John was a great guy. Then he just flat out asked if he could hire me to help out around the farm, and I worked on John Oates's farm for about two years. One day turned into two years.

He was kind of pissed when I left. I moved back to Toronto for family reasons. John was a really great guy. Hall and Oates came through town a couple of years ago. I was going to go but I was busy and didn't get tickets.

33 SAVE THE CAPS

"[The first meeting] was at Maruk's Restaurant. There might have been 15 or 20 people there. A small meeting — that got it going."

— Steve Mehlman, co-chair of Save the Caps

After playing for a few years in Washington, I was a bit of a celeb in D.C. In fact, there was even a burger joint called Maruk's in town. A businessman approached me after a game one night and asked me if I was interested in opening a restaurant. I said no. Then he asked me if he could name a restaurant after me. I said sure. There was no contract. I didn't get one cent from having my name on the restaurant. Yes, the early 1980s were a different time.

I was not financially compensated for a burger joint named after me, but when I'd drop by I never had to pay for a drink. It made for a lot of late nights and didn't really have a positive effect on the home front. What would usually start out as a good idea often turned into a bad one. Just like the Caps. When they took to the ice in the mid-1970s, it started as a positive, but by the fall of 1982, it had turned into a negative.

Selling Caps hockey had always been a problem, but things came to a head after the end of the 1981–82 season.

I may have been one of the top scorers in the NHL, but it wasn't enough to draw fans to the Capital Centre. We managed to win only 26 games that season, and that wasn't enough to fill the seats. We averaged 11,377 fans per game that year — the second highest total in franchise history at the time — but that didn't impress our owner, Abe Pollin. We weren't winning on the ice, and Pollin was losing millions because of it.

Soon after the 1981–82 season, word spread that the Caps could be on the move out of Washington. This sounded all too familiar. It was Oakland and Cleveland all over again. What I would give to play for a stable franchise. Why couldn't I just play in a place where people came out to watch?

I can laugh about it now, but I was not laughing in the summer of 1982; it was incredibly frustrating. Once again, I didn't know where I was going to play the next season — if I was going to be traded or if I would be part of a dispersal draft. With all this uncertainty around, all I could do was prepare for another season, even if I didn't necessarily know where or whom I'd be playing for.

Of course, uncertainty is par for the course for most players. You can be traded at any time. But to play for teams like Cleveland, California, and Washington, which could move or fold at any time, is a different story. But that was my lot in my NHL life. I was a guy who played for teams that just couldn't put fans into seats. Recently, I learned that I almost got a chance to play on Broadway. It was nice to hear that news — about 40 years after the fact. A guy told me that a hot rumour back in the day had me, Gilles Meloche, and Bobby Murdoch going in a trade to the Rangers early in my career. It didn't happen, but who knows what would have happened if it did? That's something to think about and ponder — four decades later — but my reality in the summer of 1982 was, once again, *This is the NHL?* For me, it was.

A dance between fans, ownership, and politicians played out all summer long. Pollin demanded that Prince George's County, where we played, give him massive tax breaks on what was called an amusement tax. He also wanted rent at the Capital Centre cut and said he needed to sell at least 7,500 season tickets and sell out the first 10 games of the 1982–83 season to keep the Caps in Washington. He said if his demands weren't met, the Caps would be on the move to who knows where.

But it wasn't Pollin who came up with the "Save the Caps" campaign — he just made demands. The fans came up with the idea, and a summer-long quest to help keep the Caps in Washington began. It was a pretty good campaign, too; they even had a Jerry Lewis–style telethon on a local television station. It all sounds pretty crazy, an NHL team holding a telethon, but this was what I, the rest of my teammates, and the fans of the Washington Capitals went through that summer.

By August 20, three days before the season-ticket sales deadline, the Caps had sold only 5,339 season tickets, the Prince George's County Council hadn't yet voted on the proposed tax cuts, and Pollin was still waiting for his demands to be met. "We are still a long way off, but we feel sure that we can do it," Caps executive director of marketing Lewis Strudler told *United Press International.*

On the night of August 24, Caps Nation learned its fate. "Save the Caps" had saved the Caps. Prince George's County voted 10–1 to cut the Caps' amusement tax. Enough tickets had been sold, or close to enough, so Pollin considered that his demands had been met. The Caps were not going anywhere. We would be playing at the Capital Centre again in 1982–83. Financially, the Caps were saved, and soon enough, they'd be saved on the ice, too.

34 THE LEFT SIDE

"I don't want to say one man is responsible for it, but David Poile and Bryan Murray changed the identity and the complexion of that organization with one simple trade."

— Greg Theberge

Once Pollin got the team's finances in place, it was time to retool the roster. David Poile, who was just 33 at the time, was hired as the Caps' general manager. I mentioned the Ryan Walter trade earlier; Poile was the guy who pulled it off. I was in need of a new linemate, but a future Norris Trophy winner, Rod Langway, and another solid defenceman, Brian Engblom, as well as Doug Jarvis and Craig Laughlin, were on their way to Washington. Rick Green also went to the Habs in the deal.

The trade changed our team radically. We had to give up good players, but it was a great move for Washington. It changed our defensive core, which was really struggling at the time.

For a player like me, having a more solid defence meant that I could go out on the ice with some extra confidence. I could try

Sarah and Jon, two of my three loving children.

a few different things knowing that I had strong defencemen out there behind me. That was something we just didn't have before.

When Walter was traded, I lost my winger, but I wasn't heartbroken. That's the nature of the business. Plus, I had played with so many different guys over the years, I believed that someone else would come along and click with me. That, however, did not happen.

It didn't happen because in the 1982–83 season, I didn't get the chance to have any wingers play with me. I was coming off a 60-goal season at centre, my natural position, but the team decided that they wanted to put me on left wing. I don't know if it was management's decision or Bryan Murray's decision, but they asked me to go to left wing. I said I would do it; I was a hockey player and I'd play anywhere. But that does sound like a strange move. Would the Edmonton Oilers take Wayne Gretzky, a natural centre, and switch him to the left or right? Would the New York Islanders ask Bryan Trottier to play the wing? Would they ask a natural winger like Mike Bossy to play centre? I figure the Caps did it because the team was pretty high on Bobby Carpenter. He was a big 19-year-old centre (6 feet, 200 pounds) that the team took third overall in the 1981 draft. Bobby had put up 77 points as a rookie the previous year, and they wanted him to play more in his second season.

In the fall of 1982, the Washington Capitals took a guy who scored 60 goals as a centre and moved him to the wing.

We started the season with 11 new skaters and a focus on defence. "Defence had always been a problem," Murray told Kathy Blumenstock in the *Washington Post* on October 2, 1982. Aside from new blueliners like Langway and Engblom, we also had rookie and future Hall of Famer Scott Stevens on the back end.

I wasn't all that fond of moving to the wing, but I sure was fond of another big story in my life: Joni and I became parents for the second time. Our first daughter, Sarah, arrived on October 15, 1982. Right away, Sarah was daddy's little girl. I don't know what it is about a little girl and her father, but the bond between us was instant. And it still exists. And like when Jon was born, I once again realized I had to take care of business on the ice if I was going to be able to take care of business at home.

I wasn't quite humming along at a 60-goal pace, but I did notch our game winner in our 10th game of the season. That seemed to get the attention of my coach. This is what Kathy Blumenstock wrote in the November 1, 1982, edition of the *Washington Post*:

> *Murray was happy with Dennis Maruk's performance Saturday. Maruk, who scored a power-play goal as well as the game winner, skated on the left wing of Doug Jarvis's line.*
>
> *"I had wanted to give Doug some more ice time," Murray said. "And I had talked to Dennis about maybe moving to left wing. He was all for it. He's been struggling, so I thought this might help get him cranked up."*
>
> *Originally, Murray intended to "flip him back to centre after maybe half a game. But he worked so well, I left him there."*
>
> *However, left wing was a quick fix, not a permanent solution for Maruk's slow start. "We'd be kidding ourselves if we said he'd be there all the time. Dennis is a centre-ice man."*

Well, I guess the Caps were kidding themselves. I played most of the year on a line with Doug Jarvis at centre, Ken Houston on the right side, and me on the left. Murray may have said I was a centre, but he played me on the left wing. Looking back on it, that move may have been my ticket out of Washington.

35 THE CAPS ARE HOT

"He made the adjustment [to the left wing] fine. I don't know if he really liked me for doing it at the time. But I think it worked, and it helped our team get better."

— Bryan Murray

By mid-December, I was still on the wing and my production was down. The team, however, was rolling. We were unbeaten in a club-record 10 games as we got set to take on the Minnesota North Stars. My desire to move back to the middle had made its way into the press. Ahead of our game against Minnesota, a headline in the *Washington Post* screamed, "Maruk prefers being centre of attention." Murray even admitted in the article, "Dennis is dying to get back to centre." But I was playing on the wing. I made my feelings known to Robert Fachet of the *Post*.

"I guess my big mistake was having a good game my first time on the wing in St. Louis. We're winning and that's the

*important thing. With the team going so well, I guess I'll
stay there for a while."*

In the same article, Rod Langway even pointed out that
the team appreciated what I was doing for them by moving to
the wing. Dennis Maruk the centre was now Dennis Maruk the
left-winger. I scored our first two goals that night for 17 on the
season in a 4–4 tie against Minny, extending our unbeaten streak
to 11 games.

We won three more before Christmas to extend the streak
to a club-record 14 games without a loss. Our final win of the
streak came against the New York Islanders. We beat the Stanley
Cup champs 5–1. I had a goal and an assist. We had never beaten
the Islanders. We were a whole new team. We were only two
points behind the Isles for the Patrick Division lead. "It's a great
Christmas present," I told the *Post*.

If that was a happy Christmas, then I got scrooged in the
New Year. When it came time to make selections for the All-Star
Game, I was listed on the selection sheet as a centre, even though
I had been playing left wing all year. Sure, I wasn't on a 60-goal
pace, but I was still leading our team in scoring. That was pretty
frustrating. I thought I deserved to go to the All-Star Game as a
winger. It didn't happen.

Once that sting wore off, I got to feel something I had never
felt before in my professional hockey career. In late February,
the Washington Capitals clinched their first ever playoff spot
with a 4–2 win over Calgary. The Caps were finally going to the
playoffs and so was I. I first stepped onto an NHL ice surface
in 1975, and now, just a few weeks away, in the spring of 1983,

I was finally going to the playoffs. We didn't exactly end the regular season on a high note, with just one win and three losses in our final four games, but the playoffs were just around the corner. Not bad for a bunch of Christians and Lions. Yes, that's right, the Washington Capitals of 1982–83 were made up of two distinct groups — sinners and saints. Or, as we called ourselves, "Christians and Lions." Regardless of our religious beliefs, we all believed in the relentless pursuit of a playoff spot.

36 THE CHRISTIANS AND THE LIONS

"The only thing I said to Ryan [Walter] and Mike [Gartner] was, 'You can have your service on Sunday morning. You can do all the right things, but don't be a hard recruiter. Don't put pressure on other guys.'"

— Bryan Murray

Let's get one thing straight: hockey players like to have a lot of fun, but not everyone has fun in the same way.

On the California Golden Seals, when the drinking started, pretty much everyone was there. On the Cleveland Barons, when things got out of hand, there may have been a few innocent bystanders, but pretty much everyone was there. Case in point: one of my old teammates on the Barons used to be a bit of a ladies' man. This guy had liberal morals and liked to put on a show, and so did his female pals. It was the '70s . . . streaking was in, and so was showing off.

We'd be on a road trip and this guy would tell us, "At

midnight, I want you guys to look out in the hallway — there's going to be a bit of a show." We'd head to our rooms wondering what the hell he was talking about. Then at midnight, about 10 or 12 guys would peer down the hall to see our teammate and his newest friend having a go. No one wanted to get caught outside of their rooms after curfew, so we'd just stick our heads out of our doors, but that didn't bother the ladies' man. He was always breaking curfew and letting the whole world, or at least a dozen of his teammates, watch him do it. He'd just look back and laugh.

Something like this never happened on the Washington Capitals. We were the Christians and the Lions.

There were a number of players on that Caps team who had found God. Ryan Walter, who had been traded to the Habs, was a born-again Christian. We had other born-again Christians on the team as well, including Mike Gartner. On the Caps, you never knew just when a guy might find God and how long his infatuation with his newfound faith would last.

We had a guy on the team named Randy Holt. He was a fighter — a hot-tempered guy who was okay with the puck but who opened up a lot of ice for me. One time, we were getting on a flight for a road trip, and Randy took his seat and opened up his briefcase. He had the usual things in there: a few papers, some undies, socks — and a Bible. Randy Holt, team tough-guy, pulled out the Bible and started reading it. And I remember thinking, *Randy Holt? It can't be.* He looks over the Bible for a few minutes and then puts it back in the briefcase. Then he reaches into another pocket in the briefcase and pulls out *Hustler*, *Playboy*, and *Penthouse* magazines. One day a guy was born-again, and the next day he was not. You question things like that.

I say either you're in or you're out. Mike Gartner was all in. Gartner was a great skater with a great shot, and he was probably one of the fastest skaters to ever play the game. One time Mike and I were rooming together at the World Championship, and I must have had a habit of blurting out "Jesus" in a very non-religious way, because he would always say, in all seriousness, "Don't use the Lord's name in vain." I don't judge people for their choices or who or what they believe in, and Mike's words stuck with me because I don't ever want to make anyone around me feel uncomfortable. When Mike told me not to use the Lord's name in vain, that stuck with me.

As the playoffs approached, maybe we were all looking for a little divine intervention. We were a team of Lions and Christians, but we were going into battle together against the defending Stanley Cup champions in the first round of the 1983 playoffs.

37 A VERY SHORT DEBUT

"He often got into it with goaltenders. Don't think that
Billy Smith and him weren't introduced to one another."

— Greg Theberge

The spring of 1983 was a very exciting time for those who had lived through some very dreary days as a Washington Capitals fan. In their 1974–75 debut season, the team won eight games. Now, finally, after nine regular seasons, the Washington Capitals would play playoff hockey. I was in the same boat as the team; for the first time in my career, I would play in the post-season.

The main problem for us was we were up against one of the greatest dynasties in hockey history — the New York Islanders. If we were going to advance past the first round, the Islanders would have to play way below their capabilities, and we would have to play way over our heads. It was a tough task.

For those of you who aren't old enough to remember or, like me, have a tendency to forget, let me introduce you to a few of the legendary names from that Islanders team. We'll start with the goalie, Billy Smith. Billy is a lot friendlier today when I run into him at NHL alumni events than he was when he tended goal for the New York Islanders. Billy Smith was a mean, great goalie. The man absolutely owned his crease. He didn't just use his stick to swat away pucks. He would swat at anything that came near him: knees, ankles, shins — you name it. As a player, you score a lot of goals from the tight, dirty areas right around the net. Well, if you were going to go into those areas to try to score against Billy, you were going to get hacked. If you were facing him, he'd whack away at your shins, and then as soon as you'd turn around to screen him or set up in front of the net, you'd get it in the back of the legs; Billy knew just where to get you, right where there was no protection. When I play in alumni games with him, he still gives it to us, and we're playing for a charity. He'll yell, "These guys are making us look bad. Let's go. Pick it up." I'll have to tell him, "It's okay, Billy. Just keep it under 10 and we'll be all right." At least he's on my team now, so I don't have to worry about him hacking away at me. But I sure as hell had to worry about it in 1983.

And, of course, if you wanted to set up in front of Billy Smith, the first step was tangling with and trying to get around one of the best defencemen the game has ever seen. Denis Potvin was a fixture on the Islanders blue line. Potvin was tough. He wasn't a big hitter, just a solid guy who was almost impossible to get around. And he was so good with the puck. You would try to stay away from Denis Potvin and not throw the puck in his corner because chances were he would get it, make a great play, and make you look bad, even on a power play — Denis was that good.

And then up front was one of the best two-way centres the game has ever seen, Bryan Trottier. I played against Bryan a lot over the years, and it was never easy. And Bryan is just as smooth off the ice as he was on it; he is a classy man, a total gentleman. I got to know him very early in my pro career when I took part in a hockey school in Victoria, B.C. He's a hell of a guitar player, too, but in '83, I wasn't worried about his strumming. I was worried about his skating and shooting.

And if Trottier wasn't enough to deal with, you had to worry about Mike Bossy as well. Bossy went into the playoffs coming off his third straight season of 60 or more goals.

So, on paper the Caps were the underdogs, and in the papers we weren't given much of a chance, either, as you can tell from what Robert Fachet wrote in the April 6, 1983, edition of the *Washington Post*:

> *There could hardly be a more difficult assignment for the Capitals' first venture into hockey's deep waters. Besides the Islanders' tradition of excellence, they have humiliated Washington in the team's last three meetings by scores of 8–3, 6–2, and 7–1.*

Robert was on to something. The Islanders hammered us 5–2 on Long Island in Game 1. But then we came back the very next night and shocked the Isles 4–2 to even the best of five series at a game apiece.

Bobby Gould led the way for us in Game 2. He had two goals to give him four on the series. I snapped a 1–1 tie with 1:13 to go in the second period when I beat Billy Smith for my first-ever playoff goal. It was the last goal I ever scored as a member of the Washington Capitals.

We returned home for Games 3 and 4. The Islanders beat us 6–2 on Saturday and then 6–3 on Sunday. Our season was over, and so was my life as a Capital. I finished the series with one goal and one assist in four games. About a week later, a few of my Caps teammates and I took off for the World Championship. We won the bronze medal.

38 BACK TO MINNY

"There were just way too many guys in Minnesota . . .
there were too many years where I swear we had 40 guys
go through the room."

— Brian Bellows, North Stars teammate, 1983 to 1989

On July 5, 1983, I was traded for the second time in my career, and once again it was a swap between the Capitals and the North Stars. I was on my way back to Minnesota. The Caps unloaded me for a second-round pick in the 1984 Draft. Just like that, my time with the Caps was over.

A week earlier, Bryan Murray had told me that he was going to put me back at centre for the coming season. We had just made our first-ever playoff appearance and life was good. Things were going to get even better: I was going back to my natural position. But Bryan's news was the kiss of death. A week later, totally out of the blue, I was traded.

The reason I was on my way out of Washington was pretty simple — the club wanted to play Bobby Carpenter more at centre. Still, it hurt. I thought I had made my mark in D.C., that I'd become a fixture on the Caps. There I was, finally, with a permanent address and on a playoff team — and then it was gone. I wanted to spend my entire career there, and I was sick of moving around. I'd had enough of the crap of moving from city to city, town to town. I wanted structure. I wanted a nice stable environment to raise my kids. I wanted to have friends and get involved in a community. But now it was back to uncertainty and Minnesota. I have to say, in hindsight, it did work out family-wise. My kids grew up in Minnesota, my son still lives there, and my grandkids live there. It's funny, all of that moving around eventually led to some of the Maruk clan finding a permanent home. I still make a lot of trips to Minny to visit my grandkids and remind them that this old guy used to be a pretty decent hockey player.

On July 5, 1983, though, visits more than 30 years down the road were the last thing on my mind. I was a North Star again. And that meant that Lou Nanne, the man whose hand I refused to shake five years earlier, was my boss again. Good times. I have to give Lou credit. He told me right away it was all water under the bridge. This version of the Stars was a deep team — they had made it all the way to the Stanley Cup Final just two years earlier and planned to use me on their third or fourth line.

In the spring of 1982, I was a 60-goal man. Then I was told I was a left-winger. Then I was told I was traded. And now, in Minnesota, less than two years after scoring 60, I was fighting for ice time. Welcome to my hockey career: I had to constantly prove myself.

There was only one way to do it: play the game that I knew.

One thing that I was not going to change in Minnesota was the way I played the game. Those valuable words, "Be a prick," stuck with me. And in the mid-1980s, if an undersized forward people called Pee-Wee was going to survive, being a prick was an absolute necessity.

39 SURVIVAL OF THE PRICKIEST

*"I don't take any credit for Dennis's career. He just asked
me a question and I said what I thought would be best for
him."*

— Dave Hutchison

Let's go through the names of a few of my foes in the old "Chuck
Norris" division in 1983–84: Behn Wilson, Jim Korn, Dwight
Schofield, and the man who gave me the valuable prick lesson
years ago, Dave Hutchison, were all on opposing Norris teams.
The Norris wasn't in full-on "Chuck" mode during my first year
in Minny, but it was getting there. A few years down the road,
I'd be playing against guys like Bob Probert, Joey Kocur, Basil
McRae, Al Secord, and a young Wendel Clark. In the Norris
Division, it wasn't survival of the fittest, it was survival of the
nastiest, and I was determined to cut my own lot of land in the
aggressive Norris landscape.

I was a little man playing a big man's game in Minnesota,

As a North Star. I kept my nasty edge well into my career.

and that's just the way it had to be done. I didn't have a lot of fights in my career, maybe 12 or 13, but I did what I had to do. I won a few, lost a few. The way I played, with that nasty edge, gave me some room on the ice. Of course, playing with some of the guys I played with helped me as well. Case in point: Willi Plett. These days, Willi would be known as a power forward. In my first year in Minnesota, he was known as a guy who could put the puck in the net and who could let the fists fly. He was a 6-foot-3, 205-pounder who had scored an impressive 38 goals with the Flames a couple of seasons earlier. In my first year back in Minnesota, his goal production went down as he racked up a Norris Division–leading 316 penalty minutes. That was good enough for second in the league.

We called him Wilbur, and when we were linemates he'd usually let me know what kind of mood he was in before the game would start. One night in Chicago, we were heading out for warm-up when he tapped me on the shoulder. "Listen, don't stir it up tonight." I loved to stir it up and raise hell — that's what I did. Wilbur was always a willing combatant; in fact, I would say he liked to fight. But not on this night. "Don't you want to fight?" I asked. He shook his head. "No. I have a date after the game." I guess his date wasn't into battle scars. I kept it clean on the ice that night, and Wilbur kept his gloves on.

But you could count on Wilbur coming right back the next game. He'd come over to me before the game got started and tell me he didn't have a date so I could raise all the hell I wanted. If someone came after me, he would happily step in and drop the gloves. I'm sure if you had the time to look it up, Wilbur's fisti-cuffs on some nights were directly related to both my hellraising and whether or not he had a date after the game.

Another guy who looked out for me back in my Caps days was Randy Holt. Randy and I first played together with the

Barons in 1977–78 and then with the Caps in 1981–82 and 1982–83. I scored, and Randy played a physical game. That's what was asked of both of us. Chances are I never would have racked up the numbers I did if Randy didn't rack up the numbers he did. In 1982–83, he led the league with 275 minutes in the box. He would always say, "Trouble finds me." He would even say it in practice. You'd skate by Randy and he'd swing his stick at your head and say, "Trouble finds me." Come game time, Randy Holt always had your back. He'd look right at me and say, "Don't worry about anything. If someone comes after you, I'll fight them."

I always knew I had guys backing me. That's why I could play the way that I did. I knew that the bigger guys on the other team may have wanted to kick the crap out of me, but chances are they wouldn't want to fight a little guy like me, so my guys would step in and things would be settled. I would be hitting everything in sight, getting my guys going, pissing off the other team, and then my teammates would come in and take care of business. It was a lot of hard work, but it was a lot of fun, too — there's no doubt about that.

These days, you see some of the bigger-name players like Ryan Getzlaf and Corey Perry fighting their own battles. In my day, that rarely happened. I was more than happy I had guys looking out for me.

40 A FIVE-YEAR LOAN

"We loved Washington so much. We had two of our three children there. I also worked in Washington as a nurse. The trade was hard, but Minnesota was a great place to raise the kids."

— Joni

The Minnesota press had basically been giving Lou Nanne hell ever since he traded me away in '78. He didn't get a ton in return, and I became a 60-goal man. When Lou got me back, he told the press, "I loaned Dennis out to Washington for five years but I got him back."

Lou may have gotten me back, but he sure as hell wasn't going to use me like I had been used in Washington. As I said, the North Stars got a man who was coming off an 81-point season and who was just one season removed from 60 goals and 136 points. And then Lou Nanne and head coach Bill Mahoney put me on the third and fourth lines.

During my first tenure with Minnesota, they got rid of me

because they were loaded with their own guys at centre. Well, it was the same thing this time around, except Lou Nanne was not going to trade me again. The North Stars had Neal Broten and Bobby Smith at the first two centre spots. They traded Smith early in the season but brought in Keith Acton. I was a North Star and I was fighting for ice time.

It was as frustrating as hell, but what could I do? I simply had to play, practise, and be ready for when the chance for more responsibility came. These days, people look at my numbers from that first year back in Minnesota and wonder what happened to me. Fans just don't understand what's behind the stats. On the Caps, I was on the first line and the first power-play unit. During my first year in Minnesota, I was on the third and fourth lines. I was not getting any power-play time, and I was playing with lesser skilled guys. When I look at my first year back in Minnesota — 17 goals, 43 assists, and 60 points in 71 games — I'm actually quite happy with those numbers.

I did get the first extended playoff run of my NHL career in the spring of '84 with the North Stars. I got five goals and five assists in 16 playoff games. We beat Chicago 3–2 in the first round of the playoffs, took out the Jets in seven in round two, and then we were soundly swept by Wayne Gretzky and the Edmonton Oilers in the semifinals. They outscored us 22–10 in four games.

I had gone from a top-line player on a playoff team to a third- and fourth-liner on a playoff team. Did the Minnesota North Stars use me correctly? Absolutely not. That's why I asked for a trade out of Minnesota at the start of my second year. But Lou had none of it. He had traded me away once and had gotten hell for it; he wasn't going to send me out of town a second time. I asked for a trade to Toronto. Nanne told me there was no way he was going to let me go to a team in the same division. I told him to work out some sort of a three-way deal but he didn't even entertain the thought. I was destined to be a third-liner at best on the North Stars.

I had to deal with a lot of adversity during my time in Minny, but I just kept going. I told Lou if that's what he wanted, then it was fine with me. He was paying me top-line money for third-line ice time. I was going to work hard: I was a pro and I would wait for my chance. I think a lot of other players would have packed it in, but I didn't quit.

From time to time, I was actually even a healthy scratch. There was nothing worse than walking into the dressing room for the morning skate and seeing the dreaded black jersey, which meant you were a spare part and would not be suiting up that night. But you have to realize that you're in the NHL and you have a job to do. That's how you reason with yourself. That's how you keep going. I just kept working. I was not going to quit.

I was a Minnesota North Star. I wasn't going to get the chance to go home and suit up for the Leafs and play in front of my friends and family at Maple Leaf Gardens. My stats from my second year back in Minny look just like the ones from my first year — a little under a point per game, 60 in 71 games, good enough for second in scoring on the team. Not eye-popping numbers by any means, but I'm very proud of them when I consider the circumstances. I scored 11 more points in nine playoff games before another season without a Cup came to an end.

41 COWBELL

It wasn't all doom and gloom in Minnesota. We had some great players who were also great guys. We had a ton of fun off the ice, too — sometimes a little too much.

We called it Cowbell.

I don't know why we called it Cowbell, but we did. It was a game the Minnesota North Stars used to play on the road. I don't know the best way to put this — and I know it will seem offensive today — but this is how Cowbell worked: We'd get together for a night on the town and we'd throw a bit of money into a hat. The Cowbell Award and its prize money would be handed out to the player who ended up with the least attractive girl of the night. (We had to witness the flirtation in order for you to be declared the winner.) Like I said, I don't want to offend anyone, but this was NHL life in the 1980s.

Chicago always seemed like the best town for the game for some reason — the Cowbell capital of the NHL. Chicago was a fun time after a game, win, lose or draw. It was a party town, with a place called Mothers that was open until five in the morning.

One guy on our team who shall remain nameless used to put a lot of effort into winning the award. He'd greet his ladies with flowers. One time he even took a girl for a horse and buggy ride; it looked like they were on their honeymoon. He came rolling by with his lady in the carriage and gave us all a big wave. It was priceless. That's where it would end, though — he wouldn't take the girls back to the hotel or anything. He would just say, "Thank you very much," and then pick up his Cowbell Award and go home. The pot could get pretty big, too — sometimes we'd put in close to $200 each.

42 A GLIMMER OF THE PAST

"If you surrounded Dennis with wingers who could play, he could really play offensively and defensively. People thought he was all offence. If there was incentive for him to get the puck, he could really create stuff, even on his own. He was one of the more creative players."

— Brian Bellows

My third season in Minny was more of the usual. I didn't play all the time, but I finished the season averaging a little less than a point per game. It was nothing earth-shattering, but once again, if you considered the fact that I didn't play on the power play and I didn't play on the top two lines, my numbers were pretty good.

We finished second in the lowly Norris Division, one point behind the first-place Chicago Blackhawks. They won our division with 86 points, which was good enough for only third in any of the other three divisions in the league. The Norris was weak. Detroit — forget about it, they weren't any good. Toronto had some good players, but word around the league was that they were mostly a party team in 1985–86. They were better off the ice than on. St. Louis was good, with players like Brian Sutter leading the way. And Chicago had a lot of talent — Denis Savard, Al Secord, and all those guys.

During that season, I was a healthy scratch on several occasions. I'd come in for the morning skate and see that black sweater. I knew I'd be watching, not playing, but I wasn't alone in the press box on most nights.

One night, I found myself up there with Kent Nilsson. He had 60 points in 61 games for us in the regular season that year. Kent Nilsson was one of the most gifted hockey players I had ever played with — the guy was just phenomenal. However, one night in Montreal, we were both banished to the press box. Kent and I looked at each other — he was a point per game guy and I was a point per game guy — but we didn't say anything. We knew, however, that we were both thinking the same thing. So we watched the game and then went out and had a few beers. We just laughed at the fact that our head coach Lorne Henning had banished two proven scorers, but it hurt on the inside. I was only 29, and I was a healthy scratch in the NHL. Did I feel secure about my job at that point? Did I feel secure about the fact that I belonged in the NHL? No, I did not — but to be totally honest, I never felt that I belonged. Even when I scored 60, I didn't feel secure.

This kind of thinking is hard on the mind. It was a tough mental challenge, but I also think it helped me to last 14 years. That's how I made it through those years in Minnesota — I never stopped fighting. I had to fight to prove that I belonged in the National Hockey League. If I wasn't in the lineup, then I had to fight at practice. I had to work hard for that next shot. In business, you have to push yourself so you don't get pink-slipped. In the NHL, it's no different. Even if I was a 60-goal man, I had to keep pushing. And when I was a healthy scratch, I had to keep pushing. I tried to look at it as a positive.

Eventually, I got my chance with the North Stars. We went up against the St. Louis Blues in the first round of the 1986 Stanley Cup playoffs. It was a best of five series, and we had home-ice advantage. We lost it in Game 1 when Doug Gilmour scored a short-handed goal to give the Blues a 2–1 win. Clearly, we were not going to win the series scoring a goal per game. We needed offence.

My healthy-scratch pal Kent Nilsson and I were put on a line with my road roommate, Brian Bellows. It didn't take long for us to click. I scored two goals and added two assists the next night against St. Louis. Brian scored two more and Kent added two assists. We combined for eight points in a 6–2 Minny win. The series was tied as it shifted to St. Louis two nights later. In Game 3, I had a goal and an assist, but the Blues edged us 4–3. The Blues were just one win away from a series win. In Game 4, Kent, Brian, and I combined for another six points. I had a goal and two helpers in a 7–4 win. This series was going to a fifth and final game. At this point, if you looked at the stats in your morning newspaper, it looked more like 1982 than 1986. I was leading the playoff scoring race with 11 points. Surely, we were going to win Game 5.

Almost 16,000 fans showed up at the Met Center for the fifth and final game of the series. It didn't take them long to jump out of their seats. Ron Wilson gave us a 1–0 lead less than three minutes into the game with his first of the playoffs. Less than two minutes later, I picked up an assist on a Brian Bellows power-play goal. The North Stars were up 2–0 less than five minutes in. But before we knew it, everything changed and it was 2–2 after one.

Our head coach Lorne Henning told the Associated Press after the game, "Maybe, subconsciously, we got up two goals and some guys started to think it was going to be easy."

The Blues were up 4–2 when we got within a goal with just under five to go, but that was as close as we could make it. St. Louis won Game 5, 6–3. Doug Gilmour had five assists that night to end our season.

I finished the playoffs with 13 points in five games. I got some power-play time, I got some major minutes, and I put up some points. It's too bad we couldn't get by the Blues. They made it all the way to the Campbell Conference final before bowing out to Calgary in a tight seven-game series. Doug finished with 21 points in 19 playoff games.

My 13 playoff points were good enough to keep me as the leading scorer in the playoffs for about another week and a half. Then that Gretzky guy jumped to the top of the scoring race. He always seemed to be doing that. Doug and his 21 points tied with Bernie Federko for the playoff scoring lead that year. The Canadiens won the Cup. That was the last time my name would show up among the top scorers in hockey. I finished my NHL career just a couple of years later.

43 LESSONS FROM A COACH AND A BABY GIRL

"Herb is an iconic legend here in the States. I think he was with Herb for a year, a year and a half or so, but that's really neat . . . it must have been pretty cool to play for him."

— Jon Maruk

"I'm very thankful for everything my parents have given me. It's kind of crazy when you think about how different your life can be when you are someone who is adopted, and have been adopted into a wonderful family. I had an amazing life and an amazing upbringing."

— Jaylee Maruk, Dennis's daughter

Long after my playing days came to an end and I was off the hockey radar, just doing my own thing in Aspen, Colorado, I was sitting at the J-Bar at the Hotel Jerome when the owner came my way. "Hey, Dennis, you see the guy with the cowboy hat? He wants to meet you. I told him about you, but I'm not telling you who it is."

Being the curious type, I moved a little closer to the mystery man. He was having a glass of wine by himself. I was looking his way, but I still had no idea who he was. He had this big cowboy hat on after all. I went to the bathroom; I was stalling. That's when it hit me. I went back and extended my hand. "You're Kurt Russell."

"And I hear you're a hockey player," he told me. Kurt asked me to sit down. It didn't take long for me to bring up one of my old coaches in Minny. "You did a fabulous job as Herb Brooks," I said. He had nailed the role of Herb in *Miracle on Ice*; the voice, the hair, the clothes . . .

Kurt said he got to know Herb and his family very well during the making of the movie. Unfortunately, as I'm sure you know, Herb died in a car crash in August 2003, just a few months before the movie hit theatres in early 2004.

Kurt and I sat there and had two or three glasses of wine. We talked Herb, we talked hockey, and we talked about Kurt's son, who was a hockey goalie. Kurt wanted to know about the ins and outs of the game, and I told him what it was like to play against the goalies in the NHL.

It was pretty surreal to sit there with the guy who portrayed one of my old coaches on the silver screen. And Herb wasn't just a coach; I got to know him in a different way than any other coach I played for during my NHL years.

Herb was hired to coach the North Stars following a lackluster 1986–87 campaign. We'd missed the playoffs and that was enough for the brass to relieve Lorne Henning of his duties. As

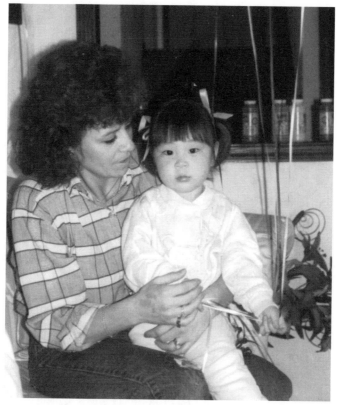
Joni and Jaylee. Raising our three children was a wonderful time in my life.

for me, 1986–87 was like any other year in Minny. I had to fight for a spot in the lineup and, as per usual, I averaged a little under a point per game: 46 points in 67 games.

By the time training camp rolled around in the fall of 1987, the team was getting its directions from the man who had coached the 1980 U.S. Olympic hockey team to a gold medal — the man who orchestrated the Miracle on Ice. This was Herb Brooks's second NHL gig. He had spent three and a half years with the Rangers starting in the fall of '81 but was fired after that team won only 15 of their first 45 games in 1984–85. Things would not be much better with us in 1987–88.

Off the ice, life was great. Jon was developing into a fine little hockey player, and his sister Sarah was, like her mom (a former Ontario champ), an outstanding baton twirler. Sarah wanted to play hockey, but I told her no. And by the 1987–88 season, Jon and Sarah had a new little sister.

That summer, Joni and I were watching TV one night when a show about children in need of adoption in Korea started. It touched me. I looked at Joni. "Wouldn't it be great to do that?" I asked. "To do that and give a child a life?"

Joni said that if we wanted to have another baby, she was more than fine with that. I had my heart set on adopting. Joni told me to look into it, and I did. I called up the agency, and soon enough, Joni and I were in a room with four other couples learning the ins and outs of adoption.

It was a very emotional meeting. The other four couples were not able to have children on their own. When we got home, I felt terrible. Who was I to adopt a child and take away the opportunity for these couples to become parents. I let the idea drift away.

A month later, someone from the agency called. They wanted to know why we didn't get back to them. I told them why. "No," they said, "that's not the case. There are more than enough needy kids out there."

On September 27, 1987, we found ourselves in the Minneapolis airport, surrounded by friends, family, and neighbours, as well as 20 or so other awaiting parents. Joni and I were about to become parents for the third time. Soon enough, an escort from the adoption agency came up to the group with a baby in her arms. "Mr. and Mrs. Maruk," she called out. We answered and she handed us our baby girl.

Up until that point, all we had was a picture. But now we were holding our new baby in our arms. We named her Jaylee Kim Ann Maruk. We loved her right from the start. She was born to a 16-year-old girl and a much older man and had been living in a foster home. Now she was with us.

When we held her for the first time, it was just like having a baby of our own. It was a really special moment. Everything we'd talked about — to give a little girl a life in America — was happening. Jon and Sarah took to Jaylee right away. She was just like a little toy to them. The Maruk clan had grown to five.

Things couldn't have been better at home, but on the ice, 1987–88 was a horrible season for me. I busted my kneecap when I went down to block a slapshot from Washington's Grant Ledyard. The injury knocked me out of the North Stars lineup, but it's also why I got to know Herb a little better than most players.

As that season went on, the losses continued to pile up. We cycled through player after player, but no matter what we did, we lost. That season, the Minnesota North Stars finished dead last in the NHL with a 19-48-13 record. The losses were hard on the players, and maybe even harder on Herb.

I was out with my wrecked knee, so all I could do was go to the Met Center and watch our games from the press box. One day, Herb said to me, "Could you come down to the room. I want to talk to you before the game. Get here by 5:30."

Those were the coach's orders, so I showed up in my suit on time. Herb wanted me to watch the games from ice level and take it all in. Maybe he just wanted another pair of eyes to see if he was missing something. After a few games, I could see the frustration on Herb's face. He did not like what was happening with his team. In fact, he was steaming. I finally said, "Herb, what's the matter?"

He let loose. "That fucking Nanne is calling me all the time and telling me who I can and cannot play. I'm the coach. I'm the one who's out there. You're out there. What do you think of that?"

I didn't know how to respond. My head coach was using me as a sounding board against our general manager. For the most part, I didn't say anything. I just listened.

"Nanne's terrible," Herb continued. "I should be the one deciding who plays and who doesn't." Maybe Herb just needed to vent, and I was there, available to listen. Anyway, that's how close I got to Herb during his one season as the head coach of the Minnesota North Stars.

I got to know Herb even more as the years rolled on. In 1995, I was the head coach of the Minnesota Blue Ox roller hockey team. I even played in two games. Herb's son was our GM, so I would see Herb from time to time.

After his season in Minnesota, Herb had two more NHL head-coaching stops: he was the head man for the New Jersey Devils in 1992–93 and he coached 58 games for the Pens in 1999–2000.

I always thought Herb was better with younger players than he was with the pros. That was where he had the most success, in college hockey and, of course, in 1980. For whatever reason, Herb, kind of like Dave King, had a hard time adjusting to life as an NHL coach. Whether or not he found success in the NHL,

Herb Brooks deserves to be the legend that he is. The way he stressed conditioning with the 1980 Olympic team started something in all sports, not just hockey. And his toughness was legendary. In Herb's mind, you didn't have to be the most talented player or the most talented team, but if you believed in your heart and in your mind that you could do anything, then you could succeed. Herb stressed that if you were willing to sacrifice and to work, then you'd find success.

It was very special getting to know Herb Brooks, as well as the man who played him on the big screen. I wish I could have helped deliver a few more wins for Herb back in the day. I did make a delivery for Kurt, though. I helped bring that $40,000 chandelier out to his place in Aspen. It was a surprise from Goldie.

44 OUCH

"I remember him blocking the shot. We were all like, 'What is he doing?' Guys just didn't do that back then."

— Brian Bellows

He was screaming and his face was turning beet red just inches away from Brian Bellows's face. He was Pierre Page, and in 1988–89, he was the new head coach of the Minnesota North Stars. Page was screaming at Brian Bellows, one of our best players, because he had made a bonehead play that led to a goal.

We were back in our dressing room for intermission, and Pierre clearly hadn't forgotten about Brian's mishap. In the visitor's room in Chicago, you had to cram yourself into these tiny little stalls. Brian was jammed into his stall and Pierre was only inches away from him as he continued to shout. Brian gave him a look that basically said, *Who gives a shit?*

The yelling and screaming didn't fly with me. There's no need to embarrass a guy in front of his teammates. If you have a problem with someone, take him into your office and straighten things out privately. We all make mistakes as players, and soon enough I would have my own one-on-one meeting with Pierre. The lead-up to my meeting with Pierre was a long one. It was over a year in the making. I started 1987–88 on the injured list. I was set to be watching from the press box thanks to severed tendons in my foot. I finally suited up for my first game two days before Christmas in 1987. We lost 5–3 to Philly. I got my first goal of the campaign a week later in a 6–4 win over Chicago. Brian Bellows and Dino Ciccarelli set me up on the power play.

The year took a surreal twist during a game at Maple Leaf Gardens. We played the Leafs to a 5–5 tie, but the score was just a footnote in the game summary. In the second period, Dino got a match penalty for a stick-swinging attack upon Toronto defenceman Luke Richardson. Ciccarelli was suspended for 10 games. Things became even more bizarre when Toronto cops charged Dino after the incident. Things were not resolved until August, when a Toronto judge sentenced Dino to one day in jail and fined him $1,000.

One week after that game against the Leafs, it was the return match back in our barn. Dino wasn't around, but this time I was wielding the lumber. I may have been getting older, but the words Dave Hutchison said to me before my NHL journey began were still running in my head: "Learn to be a prick." On this night at the Met Center, I was suddenly in very close quarters with one of the toughest young men in the National Hockey League, Wendel Clark. Wendel ended up with seven stitches. I was fine. Just over four minutes into the first period, I cross-checked Wendel right in the forehead. I got a five-minute major and I was thrown out of the game. The league gave me a three-game suspension.

"Although he may not have set out to deliberately injure Clark, there's no question that Maruk was totally irresponsible in the manner in which he checked his opponent," NHL executive vice-president Brian O'Neil said in a statement. Injuries had kept me out of the lineup at the start of the year, and now I had to sit for three more games. This season was not going as planned.

By the time a February 20 game against the Washington Capitals rolled around, I was in the lineup for only the 22nd time that season. It was my last appearance of the year. It's kind of weird that the injury that pretty much ended my career came against the team that I had my best years with — but that's life.

Grant Ledyard was a big 6-foot-2, 200-pound stay-at-home defenceman for the Caps. When you put 200 pounds behind a puck, the thing can move, and it can break a lot of things — like a kneecap. I'm a living, breathing example of that.

The Caps had the puck in our zone, and suddenly Grant Ledyard had it back at the point. He wound up for a slapshot, but there was no way I was going to let that puck get past me. I slid down to block the shot, stacking my legs on top of one another. As I slid across the ice, my left shin pad flew out of place, exposing my bottom left knee. Ledyard let a slapshot rip and it hit me directly on my unpadded, totally exposed leg. The puck hit me flush on the side of the knee.

My first thought was, *That is going to cause one bad bruise.* I had been hit before like that: it was not an ideal situation, but it was nothing I couldn't play through. I headed off the ice and went to the North Stars dressing room. At the Met Center, you had to climb a flight of stairs to get to our room. I made it up the stairs easily. I got to our room, took off my left skate and shin pad, and the team doctor had a look at things. They put an ice pack on my knee.

"Can you go out and try it?" our team doctor said.

So I took the ice off of my knee, threw my gear back on, and tied up my left skate. I had to walk down the stairs to get back to our bench. I put some pressure on my right leg and it was fine. Then I put some pressure on my left leg, and I immediately fell down. Forget about skating, I couldn't even walk. My left leg couldn't take any pressure at all.

The doc and training staff grabbed me and took me right to the hospital. They opened me up — my kneecap had to be reconstructed with pins and wires.

You'd think a guy with a shattered kneecap would have been screaming like hell as soon as that puck hit him. I thought it was only a bone bruise, and I walked up the stairs to our dressing room. How did I do this? You may call it having a high pain tolerance. I call it being a dumb Ukrainian.

I guess I thought the same thing shortly after my knee surgery — *I'll just get back at it.* I did get back at it, but not for long. My meeting with Mr. Page was just a few months away.

45 I'M DONE

*"My sister-in-law called me to tell me what had happened.
The doctor said Dennis would never play again. Well, sure
enough, he called me and he said, 'Sis, I'm going to get it
back. I'm going to get my knee back and I'm going to play
again.' I knew that he wasn't going to, but I wasn't going to
tell him that."*

— Karen Courville

My shattered kneecap essentially ended my career, but initially, I
had no intention of leaving the National Hockey League behind.
I rehabbed all summer long and had fully planned on playing for
another season.

Instead of testing my knee in the Show right out of the gate,
Pierre Page and the North Stars sent me down to Kalamazoo of
the International Hockey League for a rehab stint. They wanted
to see how my knee would hold up to the daily grind. I played
my first-ever minor league game in the fall of 1988. I didn't plan
on being a minor-leaguer for long, just a quick cameo to get in

shape. I played in five games with the Kalamazoo Wings, scoring one goal and adding five assists, before I headed back to join the North Stars.

By the time I got back to Minny, my knee was okay but by no means 100 percent. I got into my first game on December 17. We won 3–2 over Wayne Gretzky's L.A. Kings; the kid who showed up at my parents' pool in the mid-'70s was now in his first season in Hollywood. I played again two nights later in a 5–1 loss to the Canucks. Then I began a three-month-long odyssey that saw me go in and out of the lineup. Unfortunately for me, it was more out than in; I would go weeks at a time without playing in a game.

I did get to play in an exhibition game against the USSR club Dinamo Riga. It is one of the few games I played in that you can track down on YouTube. We didn't have our usual lineup on the ice for that game. Among those wearing the North Stars green and white was Mike Modano. The Stars had called him up from the WHL to give him a test against the Russians.

And thanks to the game being on YouTube, I get to watch my final ever goal in an NHL uniform. We were on the power play in the third. Neal Broten sends the puck down to Brian MacLellan in the right-wing corner. I'm on the faceoff dot on the left side. As soon as MacLellan gets the puck, I start cutting to the net. He sends me a great pass, and I go short side on Arturs Irbe for our only goal of the night in a 2–1 loss.

When they announce my goal, you can hear the crowd doing their usual screams of "Maruuuuuuuk" in the background. I'm all business back on the bench when I hear those chants rain down at the Met Center. It was the last time I heard it as an NHLer.

Sometimes things come full circle. I had the chance to suit up in Minnesota for an NHL Stadium Series alumni game in February 2016. It was a collection of North Stars and Wild alumni against the Chicago Blackhawks alumni. My old pal Lou Nanne was behind our bench.

I heard the chants of "Maruuuuuuuk" from the almost 40,000 in attendance on that Saturday when I beat Murray Bannerman for the first goal of the game. It was a nice little snap shot as we crossed into the Chicago zone on an uneven break. Unlike 1989, 27 years later I was all smiles when I scored. That day, there were no healthy scratches, no bickering — only smiles. But 27 years earlier, hockey was a business that I was being shuffled out of.

After that game against Dinamo Riga, I didn't play again until February 1 — a 4–4 tie against the Bruins. I sat out as a healthy scratch for the next two games, then managed to get into the lineup for a 3–2 win against Vancouver. And then I sat again. I spent another two games watching the North Stars from the press box. I got back in the lineup for a 4–2 loss to Detroit. I'd had enough.

I wasn't playing on a regular basis, and when I was, Page wasn't using me all that much. My knee was in good-enough shape to play, but I was at my wit's end. I had a chat with the coach, but he just told me that he was going to be using other players.

It was difficult to convince myself to carry on. I had been working my butt off and wasn't shown the respect that a veteran NHLer who had fought back from an injury deserved. I was tired of fighting for a spot in the lineup. I'd fought to prove myself since I had entered the NHL in 1975, and I guess I just didn't have any fight left in me. Looking back, I know that I could have played a few more seasons. I could have milked it, maybe taken a run at 1,000 points or something, but that wasn't my style. I decided to give someone else a chance to play. I basically thought, *You've done your thing. You've had some good years.* I decided to retire.

My decision wasn't easy. It was tough, especially because I knew I could still play. I was by no means an old man — I was only 33. When I retired, there was no massive press conference. The media wasn't all over me, wanting to know how it all came to an end.

An article in the March 14, 1989, edition of the *Globe and Mail* was headlined "Star for sad-sacks, Maruk hangs it up." The article featured a big picture of me, all smiles, back in my Seals days, and the writing was bold, cutting right to the chase. The writer, Tom Hawthorn, did not sugar-coat anything:

> *The last of the California Golden Seals has hung up his skates, putting a merciful end to 14 seasons as a sure-fire sniper on some sad-sack teams.*
>
> *Dennis Maruk was a prolific scorer whose feats — most notably scoring 50 and 60 goals in successive seasons — were often ignored.*
>
> *His crime was plying his trade in such unlikely hockey hotbeds as Oakland, Cleveland, and Landover, MD. His punishment was anonymity.*
>
> *Even the announcement of his retirement last week from the Minnesota North Stars was lost in the swirl of last-minute deals on the National Hockey League's final day*

of trading. It was a fitting, if inglorious, end to a career spent in the shadows.

I retired with 356 goals, 522 assists, and 878 points in 888 NHL regular-season games. I added another 36 points in 34 playoff games. Not bad for a guy whose teammates used to call him Pee-Wee.

I took off my No. 9 North Stars sweater. The next guy to wear No. 9 for the North Stars was Mike Modano. That's a big honour, passing No. 9 on to a Hall of Famer like Mike. He wore No. 9 for the Stars organization until the end of the 2009–10 season.

When Mike announced his retirement, he mentioned in an interview that he wanted to thank me for giving him No. 9, and that was pretty special. The first time I saw him after that, we shared a big hug. No one has worn No. 9 for the Stars since — aside from both of us wearing it at that Stadium Series alumni game. Twenty-seven years later, Modano and I were teammates again. The crowd wanted Mike to score all game long. Mike got robbed on a spectacular save by Jimmy Waite. In the final minutes, Lou Nanne even pulled me off the ice to send Mike out there to see if he could get one. It was the same old story for me, not getting enough ice time with Lou's Stars. This time around, however, I was quite okay with it.

46 NOW WHAT?

"Retirement is not easy on a lot of guys. Some are lucky and find something. It might not be what they ever dreamed about doing, but it's a paycheque and they have somewhere to go every day."

— Rick Middleton

When I retired, I wanted to get as far away from hockey as possible. That's not what happened. In fact, I didn't even leave the North Stars. I took a job selling tickets in the team's sales department. Dennis Maruk, sniper, was suddenly Dennis Maruk, suit-and-tie guy.

I walked into the office for my first day on the job just days after I retired. Was I prepared for life after hockey? I can't say I was. I'd challenged myself to accomplish one goal for my entire life, and that was to be a pro hockey player. I'd accomplished that goal, and now it was over. I had spent my entire youth chasing a dream job. I had spent all my adult life fighting to keep that job. Now I had to do something else?

Today, the NHL Alumni Association and the Players' Association help guys adjust to life after hockey. That was not the case when I walked away from the game. But it goes deeper than that. Major Junior has a scholarship program for its players now. When I was enrolled in high school in London, I didn't even show up for class. I would be at the rink or at the bar with the older guys. Education was not a priority; my sole focus was on the ice. I figured maybe I'd play in the NHL for a few years — I never thought I'd be in my 30s by the time I had to look for a real job.

But there I was, a 33-year-old ex-hockey player trying to carve out a living off the ice. Not getting an education when I was younger was a huge setback for me. I found myself seriously searching for my real interests. Did I want to be involved with the game? Unfortunately, I didn't start thinking about this stuff until after I retired while trying to sell people tickets to watch my old buddies on the North Stars.

And can you guess who my new boss was? Lou Nanne was in charge of that side of things as well. I spent my days going to meetings and listening to Lou. At times, I didn't like how Lou handled me as a player. Well, I didn't really take a shine to how he handled my new teammates in the ticket sales department, either. He would yell and scream things like "If you don't sell more tickets, I'll lose my house." He would go off on all these people who were making much less money than he was making for doing his cushy job. I wondered, *Why don't you work with these folks instead of against them.* The Stars had some great people working for them, but they were not treated great. I would tell them that they deserved better treatment, and if they didn't receive it then they should move on.

I didn't like the way Lou dealt with his people, but I actually enjoyed selling tickets. It was a riot, and it was easy for me. The clients seemed to like the fact that I was an ex-player. I stuck with that job for about a year, and then I left the organization. For the first time in a long time, I was actually getting a pay-cheque from outside the NHL. I stayed in the Twin Cities and took a job for a company called Creative Concepts. My job was to sell customized napkins to different companies, but on my sales visits, all anyone wanted to do was talk hockey. No one really wanted to hear my sales pitch — they just wanted to hear a few old stories. We'd start talking hockey, then I'd eventually say, "How about taking 5 million napkins?" They'd agree, and then it was right back to hockey talk. I'd make the sale without even having to do my pitch. And I enjoyed going around the city and meeting fans.

I carried on like this for quite a few years, living and working in Minnesota. I got my hockey fix by coaching high school hockey. And through that, I found the answer to one of the questions I first asked myself after I had finished playing. What interested me was working with kids. To be more specific, working with kids on the ice. As a player, I had attended a number of hockey schools through the summer months, and now I spent a lot of time working on the game with young players. I found it rewarding.

47 THE ART OF SCORING

*"When I think of Dennis Maruk, I think goal scorer. I
played with him during his best years. Dennis knew where
the net was. He knew how to score goals."*

— Mike Gartner

To this day, I still run hockey camps and I absolutely love it.
I even give one-on-one lessons to adults, too. Of course, these
days the highest level of the game is so much more system-based.
One thing these systems have produced is team defence — a lot
of defensive schemes. But one thing the game will always need is
people who can put the puck in the net. I'm sure you've heard the
saying "You can't teach hands." Well, I don't necessarily believe
that.

I believe goal scoring can be taught. Yes, I think there's an art
to it and that there's a bit of finesse involved. But the one thing
that is vital for goal scorers is patience — and not a lot of players
have patience. Or, at least, it does not come to them naturally.
Goal scorers know where to go and have the patience to put

themselves in the right positions to score — always. And you really need teammates who work with you. You need a teammate who gives you the puck and knows where you're going to be.

So if you have a teammate who can work with you and has the patience to find you when you're open, you'll get the puck and you'll have the opportunities to put that puck in the net. Now is when you need hands. I believe that people who aren't goal scorers can become goal scorers — they can be taught.

Right now, the game is all speed and timing. No one is teaching shooting. We have minor midget players in their Major Junior draft years, and they don't know how to take a snap shot or a slap shot. They're all fast, but they have no idea how to shoot the puck. That's not right. I teach kids at six years or seven years old that if you've got a stick in your hand, you're taking every shot. This amazes their parents. They go, "What do you mean? You can't teach my kid to take a snap shot at six years old. They can't even use it."

"Wait a minute," I'll say. "So you're not going to teach them until they're allowed to use it? Doesn't it make sense to teach it to them while they're young and basically a sponge? Even if they're not good at it, they'll learn the proper mechanics and practise until they get really good. Then when it comes time, they can use it."

That usually calms the nerves of hockey parents who have seen their kids learn only positioning, skating, and wrist shots.

I'll look at a group of six-year-olds and say something to them they have never heard from a hockey coach before: "Let's take slap shots." Then I'll show them how to put their hands in the right position. I get them to skate with the puck toward the end of the rink, and half of them fall down because they miss the puck. But some hit it and it's a lot of fun. I really enjoy that. No one else is teaching this, but that is how you learn to have hands. Just like we teach a young kid how to skate, we can teach him or her how to shoot as well.

And you can do all this while also working on the other aspects of the game. A minor hockey coach usually has about 50 minutes of practice ice time with his team, so a coach has to have a great schedule. For the first five minutes, you stretch and get warmed up. The next 10 minutes you skate. And then you work on your systems and your power play. And while one half of the ice is used to work on your systems, the other half of the ice can be used to work on individual skills, like shooting.

Even at the NHL level it should be worked on. Snipers are at a premium, so why not try to develop them. Let players work on it. But no one ever does. To me, snipers are the guys with quick hands — look at Phil Kessel. He snaps that puck off his stick so quickly, whereas other guys telegraph the puck. When you take your time with the puck, it gives the goalies time to react; snipers like Bossy and Lafleur had quick hands. And a sniper doesn't necessarily need to have the quickest feet. Look at Brett Hull — he was a guy who could get in the right spots and release the puck in a hurry.

How would I teach an NHLer to become a better goal scorer? I would watch film of his games to see what he's doing with the puck and how he's presenting himself around the net, and then we would get to work in practice. Goal scorers know the ice. They know where they are on the ice by the hash marks and circles, and a lot of times they don't even have to look at the

I'm a firm believer that any player can become a better goal scorer.

net. I always knew where I was on the ice. I knew that if I was in a certain spot and if I shot at a certain angle, the puck was going to hit the net. It may have hit the goalie, but it would've always hit the net.

I teach players that stick positioning is key. You can teach them how to use a defenceman as a screen in a one-on-one situation or how to put your stick in a certain position so that you're open for a pass but the defenceman can't stop you from receiving and releasing the puck. A lot of times, players put themselves in the wrong position and take a shot that a defenceman can block. Good shooters put themselves in the right positions and the right areas and lanes.

When you're in traffic 10 or 12 feet out in front of the net, the goalie doesn't always have a great view of the puck — that's your opportunity. If you've got a quick release, the goalie's reacting differently because he's looking for the puck and that puck's coming quicker than he thinks it is, and maybe he reacts too late. I also teach puck-control patience. Run-and-gun players don't score as much because they're going 100 miles an hour when they get around the net. Patience, head fakes, shoulder fakes, things that get the goalie moving can all be taught, and that's what I work on with my students.

Take a player like Nazem Kadri. He would score more goals if he was a little more patient around the net. Kadri has a great shot, but why isn't he scoring more? Because he isn't in the right scoring lanes or scoring positions. Get in there, find those spots — the best ones are six or seven feet from the net. Face the net with a defenceman between you and the goalie, get in tight, and move your stick to where he can't touch it. All of a sudden, you're hard to cover — you have a partial screen in front of you and the defenceman can't reach your blade. Jaromir Jagr does this. Phil Esposito did it.

We teach systems, and we need to, but you have to teach finesse, too. The game is about finesse. We don't teach goal scoring and we should. We have goalie coaches, we have skating coaches, but we don't have scoring coaches.

Kids love it, too. Coaches preach, "Don't take slap shots." I say let it rip. If you're six or seven feet in front of the net, I say take a slap shot, but I teach them the tempo. I'm not talking about a giant windup; I'm talking quick hands — it's a real quick tempo. It's like cocking a gun — *che-che* — and they kind of look at me and go, "Wow, man!"

Don't let anyone tell you that you or a guy on the third line in the NHL can't become a better goal scorer. That's a myth. I'll show you where to go, where to put your stick, how to fake a shot, and how to get rid of that puck in a hurry.

As of right now, I don't know of a single NHL team that has a goal-scoring coach — if you need one, I'm available.

48 ONE DOOR OPENS, ANOTHER CLOSES'

"He was definitely lost. He wanted to get back into hockey in some way . . . but it's hard to do. I was just hoping that it would open some doors for him. That's what his goal was — to coach and get back into hockey. He had done it at the high school level in Minnesota and really enjoyed it."

— Joni

I was in the Austin, Texas, area in the late 1990s. I had just come off the golf course and was on the 19th hole having lunch and a few beers with some of my friends. The next thing I knew, I ran into an old chum from my hockey career, Blaine Stoughton.

Blaine started to tell me about the Western Professional Hockey League. The WPHL was a pro league based primarily in Texas and Louisiana. It started in 1996–97 with six teams — two years later, the league boasted 19. It hung around until the spring of 2001.

Blaine spent the previous winter as the head coach of the

Austin Ice Bats. He told me that a number of new teams, seven in fact, would be coming into the fold for the 1997–98 season and the league needed coaches. Blaine asked me if I would be interested in coming on board. I had been coaching high school hockey in Minnesota, so I got to thinking that a move south to coach in the pro ranks might not be a bad idea. I gave Blaine my number and headed back to Minnesota.

Soon enough, he called. The owners in Corpus Christi, Texas, and in Lake Charles, Louisiana, wanted to fly me down to meet with their teams and to see if it was a fit for me. After the meetings, both owners wanted me, and each team was offering the same amount of money. I didn't know a thing about either town, but I decided I was going to go with Lake Charles. And just like that, I was a professional hockey coach. Now I had to break the news to Joni that we were back in the stick-and-puck game.

She was working as a nurse anaesthetist in Minnesota at the time and had a pretty good thing going. Of course, when I was in Lake Charles, I was not only on the hunt for a coaching job, I was scouting jobs for Joni as well. I found a couple of promising places that were looking for someone with her skills. I went back to Minny and told Joni the good news: I was the new head coach of the Lake Charles Ice Pirates and we were moving to Louisiana. I was raring to go; she did not share my enthusiasm. She liked her set-up in Minnesota.

"Does that mean you don't want to come with me?"

She said, "You go do your thing. If you like it, keep in touch." I was disappointed; I was leaving the next day and my family would not be joining me. She looked at me and said, "This will probably end our marriage." I left for Louisiana.

49 THE WPHL

"We had 21, 22 good years together and raised a family. At first we worked toward his goal, which was making it to the NHL, and he did super at it. And then he helped me get to my goal as well. I wanted to go back and do something with my career, which he facilitated. We raised really good kids. Why not like each other?"

— Joni

I didn't think I was doing anything wrong by going to Louisiana — I was just trying to get a job. I arrived in Lake Charles and got involved with the team. Even after I found a place to live and got busy with training-camp prep, I continued to look for a job for Joni. But the reality soon hit: Joni and I had essentially stopped talking.

As the season started, Joni and I drifted further and further apart. Her birthday is on December 1, but I didn't even call because I was so pissed off. Around this time, I met Kim, who also worked for the Ice Pirates. She was very good friends with the team's owner and was working in his office. She had kids, was going through a divorce, and was handling a lot at the time. Through our similar situations, we grew close, but we were never anything more than just friends.

That didn't matter to the team owner. He told me, "I see you with that girl. I know you are struggling with stuff at home." I told him that Kim and I simply enjoyed talking with one another; we related to one another's struggles at home. The owner was having none of it. He didn't want this going on under his watch. Twenty-five games into my tenure as the head coach of the Lake Charles Ice Pirates, I was let go. My coaching career was over, and it looked like my marriage soon would be, too.

Joni knew that I had made a friend in Louisiana, and she insisted that I had been fired because our relationship was more than friendly. "You've been screwing her," she said.

"No," I said.

"You're lying."

No matter how much I assured Joni that nothing physical had happened and that the relationship was platonic, she was having none of it. I had moved back to Minnesota, but after a number of intense arguments, one day she asked, "Why don't you just move back down to Louisiana? You don't need to be here."

"Is that the way you really feel?" I asked. I told her we should give it a month, maybe try some counselling.

And so Joni and I tried, but it didn't work. One night, one of the kids asked, "Why is Mom yelling at you all the time?" I'd had enough. I moved out of the house and into a casino hotel in Minnesota. I didn't stay in the hotel for long and moved in with some of our mutual friends, who were a little worried about me.

A combination of a lot of things led to the breakup of my marriage. But this was the final straw. Joni and I were together for 21 years. I moved back to Louisiana and, over time, began a romantic relationship with Kim. Kim and I were married for seven years, and we're still friends. I'm still friends with Joni, too; we have wonderful children together and we're both very close them.

My stint in the WPHL led to a lot of things: the end of my first marriage, the start of my second, the beginning and end of my professional coaching career, and, ultimately, a hockey comeback.

50 THE COMEBACK

I was a 43-year-old ex-player and ex-coach, back in Lake Charles, trying to make sense of what was happening with my life. Another turn at pro hockey was the furthest thing from my mind.

At one point in the 1998–99 season, Lake Charles ran into some injury problems. The coach Bob Loucks asked me if I could come out for a practice or two, just to get the numbers up. I thought nothing of it and laced them up. "You're doing great," he said. "Do you want to sign a contract?"

What? I was 43; of course I didn't want a contract. The coach really needed some help, though, or at least a few extra bodies.

I knew the players. I had brought a few of them in from Minnesota the previous season. They were very good players, perfect for the WPHL. I said to the coach, "You ask the players what they think. I will only sign and play if someone is hurt. I'm not going to take away ice time from the younger guys."

I thought this would get me off the hook in a hurry. I was more than happy to wear a jersey and help out at practice, but I had no interest in playing in games. Then there was suddenly a problem. The guys said, "Yeah, we want Dennis."

And so I was a professional hockey player again.

What in the hell was I going to do? I told the team, "When I'm on the ice, I'm going to be just like one of you guys. I'll be just another player, even though I'm 43. I'll pass to you. I'll try to score. I'll hit. I'm going to play hard." The young guys loved hearing that. They thought that was pretty cool.

Of course, when I took to the ice, I knew what was coming from my opponents: "You old fart. Get your teeth out." I just laughed.

"I'm 43 and you're 22, and I can play against you. How do you feel about that?"

The WPHL was a long way from the NHL. The bus rides were insane. It would take us 12 hours to get from Lake Charles to El Paso, Texas, for a game. On one road trip, we unloaded a goalie in the middle of Texas. We were on a long trip and had three goalies on the bus. The team made a trade. The next thing you know, the bus is pulling off the highway. Our management team went up to one of the goalies and told him he was traded. We dropped him off in the middle of nowhere. Someone from his new team was supposed to pick him up. Our bus driver started up our bus and pulled away, leaving a young minor-leaguer in the middle of Texas. It was crazy.

My comeback lasted for six regular-season games and another three in the playoffs. I wasn't lighting it up — just trying to survive. I ended up with two assists in those nine games. It was a tough league with a ton of fights, but I wasn't there to do that. To be honest, I really think that if I put more into it, I could have climbed back up the hockey ladder. I was 43, but I was feeling fine. My skating was pretty good and my banged-up knee felt okay. But a comeback would have taken a lot of work and sacrifice, and I just didn't have it in my heart to continue to work out. It was a lot of fun, but after that nine-game cameo, my professional career was over *for good*. And if I thought the WPHL was a long way from the NHL, my next little adventure was even further removed from my hockey heyday.

51 THE BOAT, PART II

"There was a stretch there where I didn't see Dennis for years."

— Mike Gartner

It was around this time that I ended up at the wheel of a service ship in the Gulf of Mexico.

How in the hell?

After my brief comeback, I was looking for something new. One of Kim's friends worked for a company called Devon Energy. They serviced oil rigs in the Gulf. They had four ships that they would send out into the middle of the Gulf, and they needed deckhands. I didn't know the first thing about being a deckhand, but I wasn't working at the time, so I figured I'd give it a try.

I went through all kinds of training. There was basic stuff like what a deck hand *does*, as well as survival training. If you're ever playing in a charity game against me and you run into problems, trust me, I'm your man. I went down to some town in Alabama to do my survival training and got my certificate. The next thing I knew, I was standing on a 140-foot service boat heading out to the Gulf of Mexico.

It took us about nine hours to reach a rig. Each ship had two captains and two deckhands. Each deckhand was paired with a captain for a 12-hour shift. It was 12 hours on and 12 hours off. When we were on the deck, we'd be cleaning the boat, or painting it, or doing any other kind of maintenance. The best part, though, was when you were out on the water and the rig wasn't ready for you. Basically, all you could do was sit around, and if the weather was fine, it was a pretty good gig. One thing I really love to do is cook, and the other guys I worked with definitely appreciated that.

The guys on my boat would give me a list of everything they wanted for our week out on the water, and before we'd head out, I'd go down to the grocery store and stock up on steaks, pork chops, burgers — all kinds of great stuff. Then we'd get out on the water, and if a rig wasn't ready for us yet, I'd fire up the BBQ. In the middle of the Gulf of Mexico, I'd be having the best BBQ you could imagine.

The other great thing about cooking on the back of a service boat in the middle of the Gulf of Mexico: unlimited fresh seafood. Once we'd had enough of our steaks, we'd harpoon off the back of our boat. We had a big rope with a huge hook, and we'd use red snappers as bait. We hauled in some massive fish; some of those suckers were four or five feet long, and two of us would have to pull them up onto the boat. Then we'd cut up our catch, filet it, throw some on the BBQ, and put the rest on ice.

When we weren't barbecuing, we'd be loading up these big

five- to ten-thousand-pound containers to be lifted up onto the rigs. Massive cranes would haul the containers up. I'd be on the end of our boat waiting for a huge shackle to come down, then I'd hook it up and the crane would haul the container up. If the weather was bad, it was very dangerous work. Our boat would be rolling from side to side and you'd only have about two feet between each container. I'd heard stories of people getting crushed by the containers up against the rigs.

My biggest adventure, as you know, was grabbing the wheel of one of these suckers in a violent storm. I had no idea what I was doing. Massive waves were breaking all around me. I was solely responsible for the safety of the other guys on the boat. Having the back of your teammates on the ice is one thing, but this was a totally different experience. That was when reality hit — when I realized my life as a hockey player was a thing of the past. This was my life now: trying to survive a storm in the middle of the Gulf of Mexico.

I worked on those boats for about a year. It was tough being away for a week at a time. I didn't say much about my hockey career to my shipmates. Soon enough, they discovered that the cook used to be a professional athlete. *Used to be* was the key phrase. I was a long way from 60 goals, a long way from the 1982 All-Star Game, a long way from the White House. In the coming years, I'd face even bigger challenges.

52 SO LONG, LOUISIANA

"I knew he was struggling, but I didn't know every detail.
You want to keep some of it guarded from your son. I was
always there to help and support him, but at the same time,
I think he really struggled with getting vocal about what he
was going through."

— Jon Maruk

Once more, my life was at a crossroads. After my high-seas adventures, I took a job at the L'Auberge du Lac Casino in Lake Charles. It was a busy spot. There is no gambling in Texas, so folks from the Lone Star state go to Lake Charles to gamble. I trained and became a supervisor in the casino's rewards program. Gamblers would come in and I'd help them out and show them around our place.

Kim was working in the marketing department at the same casino. She was doing very well at her job, climbing the corporate ladder, whereas I was kind of floating by. Working in the gaming industry was not my passion, but it was a job. Kim spent a lot of time going back and forth to Vegas, and, eventually, I decided to join her.

My post-hockey career was suddenly mirroring my playing career. I was jumping from town to town, looking for the right fit. Maybe I'd find it in Sin City. I had a friend who was managing a casino in Vegas, and she gave me a job in their rewards-card program. I stayed in Vegas for four months; the place just wasn't for me. I lived 15 miles away from the casino I worked at, in a golfing community made up of mostly older folks. The living conditions were fine, but the Vegas lifestyle wasn't for me, especially working from 3 p.m. to midnight. I would get no sleep at all; I'd go to work, head home, stay up all night, nod off for a couple of hours, and then drive back into town again. I gambled to pass my time. If I had stayed in Vegas any longer, you would not be reading these words. I was spiralling downward: my marriage was on the rocks, I wasn't sleeping, and I was gambling. I had to get out of that town. After four months, I decided to leave.

But where would I go next? Unlike my playing days, I could choose where I would live this time around. I had been skiing in Aspen before . . .

53 ROCKY MOUNTAIN HIGH

"He was down in Louisiana, and after that . . . I didn't know every detail."

— Jon Maruk

Kim and I packed up and headed for the mountains. Things got off to what felt like a fairy-tale start. She opened up a little antiques store, and I took a job as a bellman at Hotel Jerome, a luxury spot located right in the middle of Aspen. If you're a high roller who frequents the town, chances are you've stayed in the Hotel Jerome or perhaps visited its famous J-Bar. That's where I met Kurt Russell.

And if you wandered into the Hotel Jerome in the early 2000s and had a few extra bags with you, a former 60-goal scorer in the NHL was right there waiting to give you a hand.

I ran into all kinds of famous folk during my days as a bellhop. Joe Cocker, the singer, was one of my favourites. He used to check in under all kinds of different aliases. He was at the hotel often. His wife liked coming to Aspen to shop, so we'd always see Joe there. The first time I saw him, he had checked in under an alias, but I knew who he was and I just had to say something. I told him, "Mr. Cocker, your music is unbelievable. I love it."

"Shhh!"

We got to talking one time, and he asked about my life. I told him I used to be a hockey player. He said that soccer was his sport.

I used to take care of Will Smith all the time, too — a very friendly guy. He'd fly in on a private jet and we'd pick him up at the airport. The Aspen airport was a pretty funny place. It was just this tiny little airport, but sometimes there would be around 200 private jets there.

Working at the Hotel Jerome gave me the chance to meet a lot of people, and it got me into a lot of places. I had a friend named Willy Mannering, who I used to call Waldo, and who used to call me Mookie. Well, Waldo and Mookie used to get into all kinds of places. We knew a few people around town, and some doors would open for us. One bar owner was always very friendly to us. One night, he told me to make sure I went to their karaoke night, and that was how I met Mariah Carey. While I was telling her she was beautiful, she was likely thinking, *Who the hell are you?*

I eventually graduated from Hotel Jerome bellboy to Hotel Jerome assistant in the hotel's purchasing department. It was a nice little ride, but it was almost too much fun. I was living the life, but it was starting to take its toll. Put it this way — I used to run into Hunter S. Thompson. He would stumble out of the J-Bar, and he was always shit-faced. Well, if you're running into

Hunter S. all the time, you must be having fun as well.

Kim's shop was doing really well in Aspen. When we first moved to Aspen, her mom and dad basically ran after us when we drove out of town, so I was worried about how long she was going to stay in the mountains with me. After a year in Aspen, the lease to her shop was up, but because she was doing so well, her landlord decided to hike up her rent. That was the only excuse she needed. I told her we could move the shop to another place in town, but Kim said, "I'm going home."

I told her I wasn't going to leave — I had a good job and I was enjoying the community. Plus, I was back to coaching hockey — it was high school, but it was still hockey.

Kim's mom and dad drove all the way to Aspen and pulled into town with a big trailer. They filled it with all the items from Kim's shop — candles, antiques, clothing, everything. I told her I would stay for the rest of the year and then I would come back to Louisiana. Soon enough, my second marriage was over.

54 BROKEN

"He really went through a rough time. You really had to build him up. Every morning I'd phone him and say, 'Are you up? Are you showered? Are you dressed? Now what are you going to do today?'"

— Karen Courville

On the outside, everything looked great. I was living in a resort town, I knew the right people, and I got into the coolest places. But inside I was hurting. All I thought about was failure. My second marriage had failed, and I began thinking I was a failure as a person. I was constantly moving from one town to another, from one place to another. My post-hockey career was just like my hockey career — I was constantly on the move. Why couldn't I just find a home? Why couldn't I just find happiness?

I found that happiness, at least for a few hours at a time, in alcohol.

Like I said, everything was great on the outside. I was constantly running into a who's who of Aspen: Don Johnson, Bruce

Willis, Tim Allen, Kevin Costner, Goldie Hawn, Kurt Russell, and John Oates. I was around all those famous folk, but that doesn't make you a happy person. The first time I met Kevin Costner was at a hardware store. I ended up working at his wedding. He had a massive place outside of Aspen and had a *Field of Dreams*–themed wedding. I helped set up the place. I went out to Kevin's house a few days before the wedding and got to work. I was standing by his garage and he came rolling up in his four-wheeler, which had a bale of hay in the back. He asked if anyone wanted to help him set up the hay around the field like the movie. Someone said, "Dennis will help." So I did.

A few nights later, I was back at the Costner ranch working at his wedding. I snuck out back for a cigarette. Shortly after I lit up, there was a tap on my shoulder. "You don't have an extra cigarette, do you?" It was Bruce Willis. I said, "Sure," and handed him a smoke. "Please don't tell my ex that I'm having a cigarette, or I won't be able to see my kids for two weeks. She'll go nuts." He was talking about Demi Moore. I kept Bruce's secret, until now.

Bruce and I had a couple of smokes; we must have been out there for about 15 minutes. We started talking about hockey, then he said, "You might know a friend of mine who owns a place out in Sun Valley: George Gund."

"You gotta be kidding me," I said. "George Gund was my owner on the Cleveland Barons."

We went back into the party. I was working but still having a good time. Bruce went onstage and played with the band, and Don Johnson got up as well. Don started singing . . . man, he was terrible.

These experiences were thrilling at the time, and they're still great stories, but underneath all that fun was pain — that feeling of failure. I kept thinking about my second divorce. Why didn't anything ever work out for me? Why was I never satisfied? Why was I depressed? What was the point in carrying on? It didn't matter how much fun I had, I wasn't happy. And I wouldn't be until something changed.

55 DRIVING TO DEATH

"Finally, I just got to the point where I said, 'You know
what, hon? You're my brother. I love you. I've been there.
I've done everything I can. If you want to go out on that
bridge and you want to jump off, you go ahead and you
do that. As long as you know what you're doing and you're
totally 100 percent clear that you want to end your life.
Good night.' And I hung up the phone."

— Karen Courville

One night, I was at a bar trying to have a conversation with a few people around me, but I was too distracted by my sadness — I kept thinking about what a failure I was. And then I thought, *I'm getting out of here.* I walked home, grabbed my keys, and got into my car.

I was going to Las Vegas. I'd decided that I'd reached the end. I had had enough of my life and I didn't want to go on like this; I didn't want to have to re-group after another failed marriage.

I was a good person. Why was this happening to me?

I kept asking myself that question over and over again on that drive.

Thoughts raced through my head. Sure, I had achieved a lot: I defied the odds and had made it all the way to the NHL. But why hadn't I done better in life? I had kids who I loved, but why hadn't I done more?

I don't know if these thoughts were brought on by depression, by the amount of alcohol I was drinking, or because I wasn't eating properly. Perhaps it was the combination of all three. All I really know is I was spinning in circles and I felt horrible. I thought the only way to find some peace in my life would be by ending it.

I continued to race through the night toward Vegas. Then, for reasons I can't explain, I picked up my cellphone and called everyone who meant something to me. I called Joni. I told her that I loved her. I thanked her for all that she had given me. I called my kids. I told them that I loved them. They kept asking, "What are you talking about? Please stay on the phone." But I couldn't; I had others to call. I repeated the same message to countless loved ones during that drive through the darkness: "I love you. Thank you for everything. Things are not going my way."

"We can help," everyone said. But I was having none of it. I can only imagine the sense of desperation and hopelessness my friends and family were experiencing. I raced on. The people I cared about, who cared about me, contacted the police.

It's an eight- or nine-hour drive from Aspen to Vegas. At some point that night, I pulled off to the side of the road. It was pitch black and I had no idea where I was. I whipped my car onto the shoulder, slamming the brakes. I was done with driving.

I figured I'd have a quick snooze, then wake up and continue my journey to Vegas the next morning, where I would finally end things. I passed out.

The sun, glaring into my eyes, woke me from my slumber. I was groggy, and I took stock of my surroundings as I opened my car door. I took a few steps and stopped dead in my tracks. If I had taken just a couple more steps, or if I had driven just a few feet farther the night before, my life would have been over. I had stopped my car on the edge of a cliff. It seemed like I was on the edge of the world. I had pushed myself to the very edge, both literally and figuratively.

When I looked down over that cliff, only one thought shot through my head: *Holy shit, what are you doing?*

Maybe it was all those phone calls that helped my body release some of its pain. Maybe just peering over that cliff and seeing how close I had actually come to the end of my life brought me back to reality. Regardless, when I looked down, I instantly knew I was not going to end my life. I wanted to live. I got back in the car and headed back toward Aspen.

On the way home, I started thinking about what I had done the night before and remembered the phone calls that I'd made to my kids. Suddenly, I started shaking. I didn't stop shaking until I got back to Aspen. I got home and went straight to bed. I didn't call anyone to tell them that I was still alive. I was mentally and physically exhausted. All this time, the police were searching for me. As far as my family knew, I was dead.

I woke up the next day and got in the shower. Then my landlord called down the stairs, "Dennis, you down there? There's someone at the door for ya." I wrapped a towel around my waist and went up to see who it was.

"Are you Dennis Maruk?" asked the officer.

"Yes."

"Are you okay?"

I said, "Yeah, I'm fine. I just got out of the shower and I'm getting ready for work."

The officer nodded and said, "Okay."

It was official — I was still alive.

Looking down into that abyss had brought me back, but it didn't fix everything. I went through a tough time. Many years were a real struggle. I stayed in Aspen for another two years after that drive. By no means was I cured of my depression. I kept drinking and I kept wondering about my life. But there were no more suicidal drives through the middle of the night. I was going to fight through this and find a way to survive. I was going to try to find happiness.

But where do you start? What do you do? Some people take pills; some people see doctors. I talked. I talked to my daughter Sarah. She was one of the people I called that night on my way to Vegas. And she is the person most responsible for getting me out of that dark place. For a time, we pretty much talked every day as I tried to get my life in order. It was tough putting all my pain on my daughter, but she was there for me. My kids told me to seek help. I thought I'd be able to turn the tide on my own, but that didn't work.

I kept going back to Sarah, and the best help I ever got was from her. Whenever something bothered me, I would call her. I didn't really open up at first, but she figured out what was going on. She was so helpful as I rebounded. And the rebound is constant.

Do I have problems today? Sure, everybody has problems, but I think I'm at the point where I can have fun and still be in control. I have a lot of respect for my children, grandchildren, and friends. They helped me to realize that even though there is a tough side to life, there is always something good that comes

My son, Jon, my daughter-in-law, Hadley, and my grandkids, Miles and Owen. There's nothing better in life than being a grandpa.

from the struggle. I don't know exactly what brings the positive to all these things in life — maybe it's God.

There's a preacher from Texas named Joel Osteen. If I'm feeling down, I will open one of his books. They are very positive, and there are simple day-to-day things that he writes about that make you feel good. I don't know what the old Christians and Lions on the Washington Capitals would think about this, but I think faith helped me find the friends who are so very important to me. I think people who don't have faith in something — be it God or friends or family — struggle.

I've only felt this way for the last couple of years; I didn't understand this when I first moved back to Canada. Getting to where I am now was difficult — it didn't happen overnight.

56 HOME

*"When I think of the father that I want to be to my kids, I
want to be just like him. He's a fantastic father. He's always
been great to me. He went through a period where he had
some challenges, but it's great to see him back on his feet. It's
great to see him back in Toronto."*

— Jon Maruk

In 2008, I moved back to Toronto. It had been over 40 years
since I'd unwillingly left town to join the London Knights. I had
no intention of moving back, but a series of family events set
everything in motion.

I was visiting family in Toronto. My brother Peter was going
through a tough time. His girlfriend of 14 years, Colleen, had
ovarian cancer and was undergoing chemo. I was shuttling back
and forth between Aspen and Toronto, trying to do what I could
to help my brother.

Eventually, Colleen succumbed to the cancer. She died at her
home, in my brother's arms — that's the way she wanted to go.

My brother took me to the airport. Before I left, he said, "Colleen left me. Now you're leaving me." I told him that I wasn't leaving him, I was simply going back to my life in Aspen. I had a job and a life there. "You're never coming back," he said. He was wrong. Three months later, I returned for good. I had to come back to help my brother and to help my dad, but if I'm really honest, I came back because I had to help myself as well. I left my work at the furniture store and at John Oates's ranch behind.

I've been home for close to a decade now. Re-establishing the connection with my dad has been one of the true treasures of my return. When you leave home at a young age, no matter how hard you try, you become disconnected from your parents. Then you find yourself married with your own kids. Your winters are filled with hockey, your summers are filled with your own family, and sometimes you see your mom and dad only when you come through Toronto to play the Leafs. You love seeing your family, but that connection starts to fade.

Being in Toronto today means being able to visit my dad all the time, and that in turn means our bond has strengthened. Most of the pictures you see in this book have been sitting in my dad's place for years. He will be the first to tell you that my mom collected them over the years, but Dad has held on to them.

My dad is the quiet one; my mom was the loud one. Mom was the kind of hockey mom who would swing her purse at you if you dared to say a nasty word about her son. Dad would just sit back. That's not to say he didn't have his pre-game routines, though, which used to drive me nuts.

We laugh about it now, but I sure as hell didn't think it was funny as a kid. If I had a 7 o'clock game, I had to be at the rink by 6:30. Well, no matter the game or the distance to the rink, Dad would always decide to use the bathroom right before we left. I think he did it for fun rather than out of necessity. If we had to leave for the rink at 6:25, my mom and I would be ready to go, sitting in the car, while Dad would be sitting somewhere else. We would be going bananas. I'd honk the horn while Mom screamed, "Come on, John!" It didn't matter — Dad would take his time and come out of the house singing. But by the grace of some sort of higher power, he would get us to the rink on time, and, more importantly, he'd always get me to the rink, regardless of the circumstances.

Every Friday night, the Maruk family would feast on take-out fish and chips. One Friday night, when I was 10 or 11, my mother sent me to get the food. I decided to take my bike, and on the way back, I was hit by a car. It sent me flying off my bike, and the fish and chips went everywhere. I was really banged up — one side of my body was scraped and bloody — and I made my way home empty-handed. My mom saw me and immediately said, "Dennis, we have to take you to the hospital."

"Are you crazy? I have a game tonight."

Somehow, I convinced my parents that I'd be better off playing hockey than going to the emergency room.

"And you played well," my dad says with a laugh.

My dad was a hard-working guy. He did some time in the army and then got a job on a farm. He met my mom and they raised eight kids. He wasn't much into sports, but he played a little ball as a kid. When it came to life on the ice, it wasn't for him. "I tried to skate some, but it never worked," he says. "I don't know who you got it from."

All the Maruk kids celebrating our dad's birthday. Left to right it's me, Peter, Karen, Donna, Dad (John), Barry, Linda, Kenny, and Lori.

Perhaps what I inherited most from both my mom and dad is my work ethic. I would describe both of them as workaholics, but they never missed my games. Looking back at those old photos with my dad, tons of memories come rushing back. There I am, outside every night, under a street light, shooting over and over again. My night would not end until someone would yell, "Get in here and get to bed. You have school tomorrow."

These old pictures bring back a flood of memories about my minor hockey teammates too. I grew up playing with guys like Bruce Boudreau and Mike Palmateer. They were great players who made me a better player. I had a dream and my minor hockey teammates played a huge part in that dream becoming a reality. And it wasn't just the guys like Bruce and Mike who

My father, John Maruk, and me at an Oldtimers' Hockey Game back in 2011.

made it all the way that made my dreams come true.

Today Gary Carr is a Regional Councillor in Halton, Ontario. Once upon a time, he was the goaltender for our Rexdale minor hockey team. One night we beat the Toronto Young Nats 2–1 in overtime. A bunch of kids from Rexdale were never supposed to beat the Toronto Young Nats. We were probably outshot 48-5. Gary stood on his head.

Dad will just sit and chuckle when we talk about these things. He'll add the odd one-liner, but not much more. That's more than good enough for me. He's in to his 90s and still drives his own car. His social calendar is fuller than mine.

He talks a lot about the Leafs and, from time to time, he still talks about his young hockey-playing son. "There's a guy downstairs who's interested in sports; he's well aware of you. He's always talking to me. Always going to Junior games and downtown for Leafs games."

I know my dad is glad that I've come home, and it's such a treat to have him back in my life again.

I wish Mom was still here, too.

57 MOM

"My mother was his number-one support system; she was the biggest fan on the face of the earth. So whenever he came home, he was just like a little kid who would fall in the door and say, 'Mom, I'm home.' That's what he expected to do that day."

— Karen Courville

I miss my mom. I'm a man in my 60s and I have no problem admitting it: I miss my mom.

I suffered hundreds of losses on the ice but August 13, 1988, was one of the most devastating days of my life. I tear up just thinking about the day my mother, Anne, passed away. It hurt on a level I can't begin to describe — it hurt even more because I wasn't there.

My mom and dad lived in the Rexdale home with the pool for 35 years. When they sold the house, they downsized into a condo. Well, they were only in the condo for about a month and a half when my mother suddenly passed away. No one saw it coming.

At the time, I was living in the United States with Joni and the kids. We were supposed to leave for Toronto on a Tuesday, but we were a day behind. I called my folks and told them we were going to be a day late. "No problem," they said.

On Wednesday, my mom went to the local grocery store to pick up a few things. However, when she came out of the store she couldn't remember where she had parked her car, which was very out of the ordinary for my mom. Someone was nice enough to help her find her car and she made her way home. Looking back on things, she may have suffered a mild stroke and that's why she could not remember where her car was. When my mom got home, she told my dad that she wasn't feeling well. She said she was cold.

My mom and dad went to bed. Dad put his arm around her and they both nodded off to sleep. At around two in the morning, my dad woke up. My mom did not. She had died in her sleep.

While this was happening, we were driving through the night to Toronto. We had no idea what was going on. Remember, this was long before cellphones. We showed up at my parents' building at around 10 in the morning. We were all excited to see my mom and dad.

When we showed up, my sister Karen took me right into the elevator, and one of my brothers grabbed Joni and the kids. I was thinking, *This is great. This must be a surprise. They're trying to pull something off here, bringing us up separately.* My sister didn't tell me what was going on during our elevator ride up to the eighth floor.

When I opened the door to mom and dad's condo, all I saw was one giant cloud of smoke. My brothers and sisters were all

My mom, Anne. I miss her every day. She was so caring, loving, and supportive. There wasn't a thing she didn't do for me.

smokers and they were all there. Smoke — that's what I remember. Karen looked at me and she started to cry. "Mom died." I was in shock. I didn't even set foot in the condo. I didn't talk to anyone. I just took off. I was my mom's pride and joy; my mom loved all of us, but she and I had such a special relationship. And now she was gone. I had no idea what to do.

When I got to the main floor of the condo, I bolted through the doors and I ran and ran and ran. And I cried. I had no idea where I was going. I was running and I just kept going. I returned to the condo about an hour and a half later. It was then that I realized that my wife and kids must have been wondering, *What the hell is going on?* We had a proper funeral for my mom and laid her to rest — but it still hurts so much.

There are things from that time that are stuck in my head. Everyone in my family loves to play cards. My son, Jon, was so excited to see his grandma on our trip up to Toronto. On previous family get-togethers, my mom was always trying to teach Jon how to play cribbage, but he was just a little guy and he couldn't count. He took it upon himself to correct that. His school would visit the fire station, and for some reason the firemen taught him how to count, and I worked with him a little bit as well. On our drive up to Toronto, he was so excited. "Dad, I can't wait to show Grandma how to count crib," he said from the back seat. But he never got that chance. We had to explain the news to him and Sarah that Grandma wasn't here anymore.

At the funeral, Jon asked, "Dad, can I put something in the casket?" I looked at him and said, "Sure, put whatever you want in there." He told me he wanted to put a deck of cards and a crib board in the coffin for his grandmother. It was devastating.

My mom and I were so tight because I left home at such a young age. When I was a kid, 13 or 14 years old, I'd always take care of things around the house. I wasn't the oldest kid in our family, but it was just something I did. While both of my parents were at work, I'd make sure the house was clean and that my brothers and sisters had lunch. No one asked me to do it, but I made sure that by the time Mom or Dad got home from work, there wasn't a mess around. I'm sure my motives weren't totally selfless; I knew that if I wanted a hockey stick, Mom and Dad would likely get one for me if I put in a few extra hours around the house.

They were my biggest fans. They never missed a junior game. Mom was the voice of the family, and she was always there to let me know how proud she was of me. Looking back, I'm so happy she got to realize just how much her support meant to me. Having them in D.C. for the All-Star Game in 1982 was a huge honour, and it was very cool to have them around for the festivities. There I was, their son, front and centre, dining with the president. We had a film crew following us around that week, and Mom and Dad got a lot of face time on TV. They even filmed Mom, Dad, and me driving to the rink in a big Cadillac. It was a very special time for me, not only as a hockey player but as the son of Jon and Anne Maruk.

I miss my mom, and I know I'm lucky to still have my dad, but I've also told you about how busy he is. The Caps were in Toronto the other night to play the Leafs, and I asked my dad if he wanted to go to the game with me. He had to pass — he had a date.

I took my brother instead.

58 THANK YOU

"At one point, he was so down that he tried to take his own life. He called me and I talked him out of it. I stayed on the phone with him, and I'm so glad I did. It was a lot of listening and letting him know that even in his deepest, darkest times, I love him and I couldn't imagine life without him."

— Sarah

How do you say thank you to the woman who saved your life? My daughter Sarah saved mine. She helped me through my depression over the years. I put her through so much during and after that drive to Las Vegas.

In the months and years that followed, I didn't seek professional help. Sarah was my sounding board. It was so hard for me to heap all my problems on someone I loved so much, but Sarah took it all in. She listened to every word as her father poured his heart out. It could not have been easy — she is the reason I am writing these words.

She called me every day to check up on me. Every day. I finally got to say thank you to her at her wedding.

It was hard, but I got up and made a speech in front of all the guests at her wedding. I wanted to let everyone know what a wonderful woman Sarah is. And I wanted to let everyone know that it was my daughter who saved my life. I opened up at that wedding and told everyone my story. How I was at the edge and Sarah brought me back — that she saved me. Most people at the wedding had no clue that I had been in such a dark place. All they knew was that I was Sarah's dad, the old hockey player.

I got a lot out of my system that night. Many people came up to me afterward to let me know they thought what I'd said was moving. For me, it was very liberating. I had a great time that night. After I got all of that pain out of my system, after I got to thank my daughter for saving my life, I felt like a free man. I went out on the dance floor and I had a great time.

I didn't want to be the centre of attention at my daughter's wedding. That day was for Sarah and her husband. I just had to tell everyone how important Sarah is to me. I didn't want to take anything away from them; I just wanted to say thank you.

Sarah and I don't talk every day now, but we still talk a lot. When I send her a card on her birthday I never think that's enough. I want to send her a best friend card, too. Thank you, Sarah.

I'm so proud of all of my kids. Each one has taught me something special. Sarah lives in Miami now. She's a long way from home. So is Jaylee, who is in Hollywood. Jon's still in Minnesota.

When I was playing, I got a chance to be a pretty hands-on dad. I grew up in a large family, and when Jon arrived I was ready

With Jaylee, Jon's wife, Hadley, Jon, and Sarah on Jon's wedding day. I was so proud to be there, but even more proud to be the dad of my beautiful kids.

to spend as much time with him as possible. Growing up in my house, my dad was always pulled in a lot of different directions. I was determined to play a major part in Jon's life.

Jon was always with me at the rink, and the guys on the Caps and North Stars just loved him. He developed into a great little hockey player as well. Just like his old man, he was always his team's leading scorer and MVP. He may have been great on the ice, but early in his hockey career I was nowhere near in the running for the World's Greatest Hockey Dad Award.

To be honest, I was a *lousy* hockey dad. The pro game was all I knew. I was in a strange land when it came to the uber-sensitive world of minor hockey. One game in particular stands out. Jon was about 11, and in my mind he was dogging it. A whistle went and the players lined up for a faceoff, and Jon was at centre. The rink was deadly quiet. At this point, I took it upon myself to impart some wisdom to my kid. I was never shy about being vocal at the rink, and this time was no exception. "Hey, number 9," I yelled across the quiet ice. "If you're not going to start working and hustling, you might as well head to the dressing room. We can public skate on Saturday." Jon just turned around and stared.

After the game, Jon asked me how I thought he played. "You could have done better," I said. I wanted Jon to follow in my footsteps. I wanted him to play in the NHL one day. But he was just 11.

"Dad, I'm sick and tired of you telling me negative things," he said. "Why don't you tell me the positive things you see out on the ice. I'm always going to make mistakes." And then he began to cry.

Jon may not know it, but that moment changed me. And it changed how I looked at the game. It changed how I looked at kids on the ice and parents in the stands. It changed the way I behaved. After that, I talked only about the positives. And what do you know, Jon became an even better player.

He was a fantastic player, in fact. I wanted him to go and play for the London Knights in the OHA, but his mom wanted him to play college hockey. Jon played NCAA Division I in, of all places, Anchorage, Alaska. I couldn't believe it. He had his heart set on playing in the WCHA and moved to Alaska in the fall of 1997. He stayed in Alaska for two years before he transferred to Notre Dame. He graduated with an economics degree in 2002.

I swear he could have played in the NHL. He played in the minors for a little bit before he packed it in. He got a job offer from a company in Minnesota that he just couldn't pass up. He was a great two-way player. I was faster, but he was stronger. He had an all-around game; something I didn't have.

He may never have played in the NHL, but he had a first-rate education to lean on, something I never had either. He and his wife, Hadley, have given me the greatest gift of all, two beautiful grandchildren named Owen and Miles.

When I wasn't hustling Jon to rinks I would be driving Sarah and Jaylee all over town, often to baton twirling competitions. As for Jaylee, you may have already seen her on the big screen. She's an actress in Hollywood and has been on the hit show *Scorpion*. In fact, she does a bit of everything. She sings and teaches archery as well.

In addition to all of this, Jaylee speaks five languages; she's fluent in French, Italian, German, Japanese, and English.

It makes me so proud to see the life that Jaylee leads; she's an incredible story.

I'm so proud of all my children. And it is true — no matter how old you or your kids get, you never stop being a dad.

59 WHAT DOES 60 MEAN?

"Can you imagine if Dennis scored 60 goals in a Leafs
jersey? He could sure put the puck in the net. If he scored 60
as a Leaf, that would have been unbelievable; he would be
sitting on Legends Row."

— Bill Derlago, 158 career goals as a Leaf

I spent my childhood years dreaming of being a professional
hockey player. It's all I wanted. That, and, of course, playing for
the Toronto Maple Leafs.

I never got to play for the Leafs, but it wasn't from a lack of
trying.

When I was a pro, I tried to get traded to Toronto, but it
never worked out. Who would have wanted to play for the sad-
sack Leafs of the 1980s, you wonder? Well, I did. Maybe it all
goes back to the fact that I was supposed to play in the Gardens
for the Marlies but got traded to London. That started a hockey
odyssey that saw me play in the Gardens only as a visitor.

If there's any one thing I regret not achieving, it's that I never got to play for the Leafs. Even when I turned pro, I still cheered for the Leafs. And I still cheer for the Leafs to this day. I'm a kid from Rexdale, after all. I was born to be a Leafs fan.

I can only imagine what my life would have been like if I had scored 60 goals in a Leafs uniform. They've never had a player score 60 in a season. Rick Vaive was the first Leaf to score 50; he scored 54 the same year I scored 60. Rick is still a Leafs legend, and deservedly so. I wonder, though, what would have happened if I'd scored my goals for the Buds.

I'm sure that if I was wearing a Leafs uniform there would have been more than one article about my 60th in the *Globe and Mail*. Sure, I scored my career best the same year Gretzky scored 92, but I still think 60 in a Leafs uniform would have garnered a fair share of ink in the spring of 1982. I'm also sure that if I scored 60 in a Leafs uniform, no one would be asking, "Who's that guy?" when they look at the list of hockey's 60-goal snipers. But still, 60 does define me. Once people figure out that I scored that many goals in a season, they want to talk about it. Not long ago, I ran into one of the Leafs' equipment guys at their practice facility. I've known the guy for a long time. He introduced me to two of his buddies. They said the usual, "Nice to meet you . . ." Then my buddy told them I was a 60-goal man and the conversation took off. That's the way it is. And that's fine.

Would I like the Capitals to make more of a big deal out of my scoring 60? Sure, who wouldn't want that? But the Caps aren't exactly tied to their history the way the Canadiens, Leafs, or Bruins are. Denis Savard, who I run into at a lot of alumni events, once asked, "Why don't you do more stuff for Washington? They should be flying you in and inviting you to town for all of their events." I guess it comes down to dollars and cents. If I lived in the D.C. area and was only a drive away from their home games, I'm sure I would be more involved. Still, I'm happy to go to the Verizon Center any time. What old guy wouldn't want a crowd applauding him for something he did over 30 years ago?

60 NOW

"I'm thrilled for him. He just seems to be in a much better place, having fun with our kids and grandkids. He's playing a big part. He needed to find a purpose again, and his identity has always been hockey. He's got a lot to offer that way. He's got a great personality. He's great with fans and people."

— Joni

"The Hawks and the Wild had that outdoor game. To be able to bring my four-year-old in a number 9 Maruk jersey was a thrill. There was about forty thousand people there, the place was packed, and Dad went and scored the first goal. His grandson went ballistic. It was pretty cool. I was equally as happy for my dad. He walked out of there with a pretty big smile on his face."

— Jon Maruk

"Dennis is such a nice guy. We run into each other at some

of those charity deals, and he's always going out of his way
to check in and see how we're doing. He's always got a smile.
He's always in a good mood. One of the things that really
stuck out to me is that I think he feels fortunate and lucky to
do what he did."

— Mike Modano, Hockey Hall of Famer,

former Minnesota teammate

I fought every day during my 14-year National Hockey League career to prove that I belonged. My career ended almost three decades ago, but I am still fighting. My life after hockey has not been easy. I did not have a smooth transition into retirement. I tried to knock on a few doors and get back into the game, but I couldn't get a sniff at a job in the pros. There's a long list of people I contacted while looking for a job, but the doors never opened for me, and a couple of marriages ended in the process.

I still communicate with my first wife, Joni. She's Grandma and I'm Grandpa. We talk and keep it positive — nothing negative. I also still talk to my second wife, Kim; we have a good understanding for one another. But there were issues with both marriages. I was in a long, downward spiral after my hockey career. I don't think I realized how dark a place I was in until I walked to the edge of that cliff on my way to Las Vegas. That was when the reality of my life after the game — the struggle — really hit home. I could have fallen over the edge. Everything could have ended right there. Looking down opened my eyes to my life.

I've tried to change ever since that night. I've tried to recognize and emphasize the positive things. I have three beautiful children: Jon, Sarah, and Jaylee. I am blessed with two grandkids, Miles and Owen. Little Miles even has proof that his grandpa played in the NHL; he was at the Stadium Series alumni game in Minnesota. Scoring the first goal of the game was a thrill, but having Miles there to see it really made my day. When I'm having a rough day, I remind myself that the kids need their grandpa around.

During the process of writing this book, I got another reminder just how precious life can be. In December 2016, I was following up on an old medical file from a disability claim against the state of California. I took the file to my family doctor here in Toronto. My doctor asked me to come in for a few tests; I figured it was pretty routine stuff. The old file had said that the left side of my heart was thicker than the right side. My doctor wanted to check it out. So we went ahead and did a number of tests, including a stress test. When I pushed real hard on the treadmill, my numbers weren't exactly what they wanted to see, so they asked me to do an angiogram. On December 10, 2016, they knocked me out and put dye in my heart to see what was going on in there. They found that 90 percent of the main artery was blocked on the left side and the other arteries were blocked, too.

They woke me up from the test and gave me the news; I needed open heart surgery — a quadruple bypass. They told me I had a heart condition that is referred to as the widow-maker. I was in good shape, but I could have had a massive heart attack and dropped dead at any second. I didn't have a single symptom — no chest pains, nothing. But my life could have ended just like that.

Hockey continues to take me around the world. Here I am with a few Caps alumni, looking very important in the office of the president of the Czech Republic.

I was terrified. When I had my pre-op, the doctors and nurses told me I was lucky to be alive. It's a good thing I was in shape from all the hockey I still play. They said my heart was so strong that it didn't need a lot of blood. If it wasn't as strong as it was, it could have just clogged right up, and my heart just would have stopped. Game over.

On January 23, 2017 surgeons ripped my chest apart and fixed my heart. When I woke up the doctors asked me, "Do you remember what you said before we put you out?"

I told them I didn't. They told me: "You asked where Freddy was? Who's Freddy?"

"Freddy Krueger," I said. I told them to make sure he had his scissors sharp when they cut through my sternum.

My children came to visit me during my surgery and recovery, which wasn't easy. Some people are out of the hospital in three days. I was in for another ten. They had to give me more blood on the fifth day; my hemoglobin was low and a lot of my numbers were high.

You struggle through the surgery and you handle what is thrown at you as it comes, but when you start to heal and feel better, you think, "Wow. I'm lucky to be alive. I'm lucky to be here." I have to really thank whoever's up there looking after me — it might be my mom.

But I'm still here, and I'm back on the ice. Physically, at least, it seems like the surgery didn't even happen. In May 2017, I played hockey in Astana, Kazakhstan, with a group that included Igor Larionov, Brian Propp, and Ken Dryden, as part of the Canada 150 celebrations.

When I do hockey events now, I tell guys that if you feel chest pains and you think you're just sick, maybe you've got the flu or heartburn, you have to go to the hospital — those are symptoms of heart problems. And a lot of guys with symptoms like that don't go get checked out and they drop dead. You don't know if your arteries are clogged unless you go in and get it checked. So I tell everybody about what I went through.

If you want to live a long time, you need to take care of yourself. You know, I have had some wild times. I don't drink as much as I used to. It's a change, and it has to do with getting older. It's another chapter of my life that I certainly didn't want to deal with, but it happened. They cut me open and I'm still here.

Now I've got a new lease on life. You feel like you've got

Me, Gordie Howe, and Lanny McDonald at the ScotiaBank ProAm Game for Alzheimer's.

a second chance at life when a surgeon tells you you could have 20-plus years left when you had almost ran out of years completely.

I would love to be retired by the time I'm 65, maybe even sooner. My goal is to be able to travel around and visit my grandkids for three months every year; it's hard to kick the travel bug you get from playing hockey around the country. People ask me what I miss most about the game and I say the travel. Maybe some guys are happy to have all those air miles out of their lives, but I truly enjoyed that aspect of the game.

I guess I'm still a hockey player. That's what I've always been defined as. Maybe during all those years I spent out of the game — working as a bellhop, farmhand, and furniture-store manager

— I was trying to be more than just a hockey player. Or maybe I was just trying to get over what had been a painful transition to my post-NHL life.

I say I'm still a hockey player because I still play the game. I don't make money doing it anymore, but I'm on the ice all winter. I play in old-timers' games in front of hundreds in tiny rinks in Newfoundland and tens of thousands in outdoor stadiums in Minnesota. And whether I'm playing in front of hundreds or thousands, I'm still smiling.

Fans may not be as quick to recognize me as they were when I was scrambling in front of the net for the Washington Capitals. And even though the Fu Manchu is gone, I like to think the hands are still there. I love to set teammates up for goals. It's like watching their dreams come true when they score. A lot of times, we will play with older gents who dreamed of playing in the NHL as kids. If I can set them up for an open net and make their night, I'm especially happy to do it. Sometimes on the bench a guy will say to me, "You know, I've never had a hat trick." I'll say, "Come on my line, stand in front of the net, and I'll just slide it over." I get excited by things like that.

I play more now than I ever have. Being on the ice is good for me. Joni got remarried to a very nice man, and they are involved in the racehorse industry. One time, he and Joni were up here in Toronto, and he said to me, "I think Toronto's good for you." He's right. Will I ever move back to Aspen or Minnesota? I don't know; Toronto is my home base. And like I said, even today I'm all over the place, from Newfoundland to Minnesota to Western Canada. For some reason, when I'm structured, anchored down in one place, trouble finds me. Today, I feel like I'm on the move,

I am so happy with my decision to move to Toronto. I was fortunate to meet Suzan Cameron, a lovely, caring, and beautiful woman.

like I was as a player. I've got close friends here, though. And if I have issues, I can talk to my friends and to my family. That's something I didn't have for a long, long time.

My story is not about being in the elite 60-goal club — it's about overcoming challenges in your life. Everybody wants to find happiness. Sometimes I've had it; sometimes I haven't. I've been at the top. I've been an All-Star on home ice in front of my mom and dad. And I've been at the bottom, on a drive toward my own death that night in the desert. But I put the brakes on that drive. That was the bottom. But it gave me an opportunity to realize just how much I was loved. That changed me. I can't thank my children Jon, Jaylee, and Sarah enough for all their love and support that destroyed the demons. That was the bottom. Since then, it's been up.

These days, I live in a condo in the west end of Toronto, not that far from where I grew up with my seven brothers and sisters in Rexdale. I'm in a beautiful, loving relationship with Suzan Cameron, a woman I recently met. Things have been very rewarding since I've been back home; I love that I've gotten to know my hometown again.

I've had the opportunity to see my brothers and sisters. I skate every Monday night with a group of 40 guys. My buddy Mike Donia dragged me out there. When I showed up, I was a stranger, now I have 40 new friends. We always have an awesome time, and we chat about everything. That's where I met my great friends Chris, Michael, Matthew, and Mark Bratty and Paul Lonergan. And then there's Carlo and Trish Matulich. I met Carlo when I first moved home, at the Hockey Hall of Fame Awards Banquet. Since we met, they have been my best friends. For a long time, I kept my pain inside. But now I'm free. I'm finally happy and relaxed. I used to be afraid of what was ahead of me in life.

That ride through the desert jolted me back to life. Years later, my heart scare was another reminder of just how precious life is. I didn't ask for that reminder, but it happened. Both cases, the drive and the surgery, could have been The End for me. Now I'm thrilled to say my story is to be continued . . .

ACKNOWLEDGEMENTS

First and foremost, I would like to thank my successful writer and friend, Ken Reid, for putting countless hours into the project and for making this all happen. I definitely need to thank ECW and Laura Pastore for believing in my story and putting this book together.

To my mentor, NHL Hall of Famer Marcel Dionne, for proving to the hockey world and me that a small man could play this great game of hockey. I personally thank you, Mr. Dionne, for the drive and determination to be successful and to follow in your footsteps. I'm glad to call you my friend.

To all my teammates, coaches, trainers, and competitors: thank you for helping me reach my goal and for the wonderful comments from my peers — you'll never be forgotten.

I cannot forget to thank the media for their coverage of me throughout my career.

What can I say to my three brothers, Peter, Barry, and Kenny, and my four sisters, Donna Karen, Linda and Lori. Thank you for your love and for inspiring me to succeed.

Jon, Jaylee, and Sarah: thank you for seeing me through the tough times and for listening and caring for my safety.

To my dad, John, and my mom, Anne: I love you!

— Dennis Maruk

First off, a huge thank you to Dennis. The first time we talked was when I called him out of the blue for my first book, *Hockey Card Stories*. A while later, I was asked if I would like to write a book with him. We decided to meet for a quick lunch. That lunch turned into a four-hour interview session, our first of many. Now, a couple of years later, we've got a book. Thank you, Dennis, for letting me into your heart and mind and for being so open about the good and not-so-good times.

A massive thank you to the countless people who picked up the phone and assisted with this project. Whether it was Dennis's family or his teammates and opponents, dozens of people were more than happy to speak to me to help put this book together. Your insight was immeasurable.

I can't thank Laura Pastore and Michael Holmes at ECW enough for their patience with this project. They are true pros, along with Jack, David, Crissy, Emily, Sarah, and everyone else on Gerrard St. East. Thank you for backing and supporting this project.

The man, myth, and somewhat-legend Brian Wood is our literary agent and believed in this project from the start. Thank You, Brian, for going to bat for Dennis and me.

Thanks to Lance Phillips and Mike deCourcy, who transcribed several hours of interviews. Also thanks to Jeff Marek, who is always so supportive of my writing, Steve Dangle, Tim and Sid, the BOB, my colleagues and bosses at Sportsnet, Osmak, Moynes, Mom and Dad, Paul Patskou, Azzo, Marchese, Leo Burke, Troy Shanks, Peter, Katie, and countless others who helped with this project.

And thank you to my wife, Ash, for her patience and support. It could not have happened without you. And to my two boys for hanging out with Dad while he pecked away the computer. Here's another one Cobs and Lou can take a peek at one day.

— Ken Reid

GET THE EBOOK FREE!